Ellen Creathorne Clayton

Female Warriors

Memorials of Female Valour and Heroism, from the Mythological Ages to the Present Era. Vol. II

Ellen Creathorne Clayton

Female Warriors
*Memorials of Female Valour and Heroism, from the Mythological Ages to the Present Era.
Vol. II*

ISBN/EAN: 9783337014612

Printed in Europe, USA, Canada, Australia, Japan

Cover: Foto ©ninafisch / pixelio.de

More available books at **www.hansebooks.com**

FEMALE WARRIORS.

MEMORIALS OF

FEMALE VALOUR AND HEROISM, FROM

THE MYTHOLOGICAL AGES TO THE PRESENT ERA.

BY

ELLEN C. CLAYTON

(*MRS. NEEDHAM*),

AUTHOR OF

"QUEENS OF SONG," "ENGLISH FEMALE ARTISTS," Etc.

IN TWO VOLUMES.

VOL. II.

LONDON:
TINSLEY BROTHERS, 8, CATHERINE STREET, STRAND.
1879.

[*All Rights Reserved.*]

CONTENTS

CHAPTER I.

Page

Captain Bodeaux, Female Officer in the French Army—Christian Davies, *alias* Mother Ross—Female Soldier in the 20th Foot—Women of Barcelona—Hannah Snell, Private in the Line and Marines—Phœbe Hessel, Private in the 5th Regiment—"Paul" Daniel, a Female Recruit—Hannah Whitney, and Anne Chamberlayne, Female Sailors—Mary Ralphson—Miss Jenny Cameron—"Pretty Polly Oliver"—Anne Sophia Detzliffin, Prussian Female Soldier—Madame de Drucourt (Siege of Louisbourg)—Madame Ducharmy (Capture of Guadeloupe)—Chevalier d'Eon—Deborah Samson, Private, and Molly Macaulay, Sergeant in the American Revolutionary Army—Elizabeth Canning—Catherine the Second of Russia and the Princess

Daschkova—Doña Rafaela Mora, Female Captain in the Spanish American Service (How Nelson Lost an Eye)—Female Sailor on Board Admiral Rodney's Ship . . . .   Page 1

CHAPTER II.

THE FRENCH REVOLUTION—The Furies—Rose Lacombe—Théroigne de Méricourt—Madame Marie Adrian (Siege of Lyons)—Renée Langevin—Madlle. de la Rochefoucault—Madame Dufief (War in La Vendée)—Félicité and Théophile de Fernig, Officers on Dumouriez's Staff — Mary Schelienck — Thérèse Figueur, French Dragoon—"William Roberts," the Manchester Heroine, Sergeant in the 15th Light Dragoons and the 37th Foot—Mary Anne Talbot, Drummer in the 32nd, Cabin Boy on board the Brunswick, and Middy on board the Vesuvius—Highland Soldier's Wife at the Storming of New Vigie — Susan Frost — Peggy Monro (IRISH REBELLION)—Martha Glar and other Swiss Heroines—Queen of Prussia at Jena—Marie Anne Elise Bonaparte, Princess Bacciocchi—Maid of Saragossa—Manuella Sanchez, Benita, and other Heroines of Saragossa—Spanish Female Captain—Mrs. Dalbiac (Battle of Salamanca) — Ellonora Prochaska, Private in Lutzow's Rifle Corps—Augusta Frederica Krüger, Prussian Soldier—Louise Belletz, French Artillery Soldier— Mrs. Heald and Mrs. Helm (Chicago Massacre) .   43

CHAPTER III.

Bobolina (GREEK REVOLUTION)—Doña Maria de Jesus, Private in the Brazilian Army (War of the Reconcave)—Russian Female Soldiers—Juana de Arieto (Civil Wars in Spain, 1834) — Anita Garibaldi—Appolonia Jagiello (Rebellions in Poland, 1846-48), and Vienna and Hungary in 1848)—Bravery of the Croatian Women—Countess Helene St.——, a Hungarian Patriot—Garde Mobile—Louisa Battistati (Milanese Revolution, 1848) —Fatima, a Turkish Commander (Russian War)—Lady Paget (Attack on the Mamelon, 1855 — Miss Wheeler (Cawnpore Massacre)—Ex-Queen of Naples—Polish Insurrection—Mdlle. Pustowjtoff, Adjutant to Langievicz—Female Chasseurs— Female Lieut.-Colonel in the Mexican Army—Civil War in America — Female Privates in the Potomac Army—Female Lieutenant and Privates in the Army of the West—Mrs. Clayton, Private in the Federal Army—Emily——, Private in the Drum Corps of a Michigan Regiment—Female Confederates at Ringgold, Chattanooga — Mrs. Florence Bodwin — Female Mulatto Sergeant—Native Contingent in New Zealand — Herminia Manelli, Corporal of Bersaglieri (Battle of Custozza, 1866)—Lopez's Amazons—Cretan Amazons—Women of Montenegro—Maria L——, French Sergeant—Female Brigands—German Order to reward Courage in Women—Minna Hänsell (Franco-Prussian War) —Miss Jessie C. Claffin (American Colonel)   96

Page

CHAPTER IV.

Indian Amazons—Cleophes, Queen of Massaga—Moynawoti, Queen of Kamrup — Ranee of Scinde—Sultana Rizia—Gool Behist—Booboojee Khanum and Dilshad Agha, Mother and Aunt of a King of Bijapur — Durgautti, Queen of Gurrah — Khunza Sultana, Regent of Ahmednuggur—Chand Sultana, Regent of Ahmednuggur—Nour Mahal, Empress of Hindostan — Princess Janee Begum — Juliana—Madam Mequinez, Colonel in the Service of Hyder Ali Khan—Begum Somroo, General in the Service of the Emperor Shah Aulum and Grandmother of the eccentric Dyce Sombre—Begum Nujeef Cooli—Mrs. W., Native Wife of a British Sergeant in India —Lukshmi Baee, Ranee of Jhansi (Indian Mutiny)—Female Mutineer captured before Delhi, 1857—Female Guards in the Zenanas of Indian Princes—Begum of Oude—Bantam Amazons . . . 138

CHAPTER V.

SOUTH AFRICA.

Judith, Queen of Abyssinia — Workite and Mastrat, Gallas Queens—Shinga, Queen of Congo—Mussasa, Queen of Matamba—Tembandumba, Queen of the Jagas—Amazons in Dahomey . . . 185

FEMALE WARRIORS.

I.

Captain Bodeaux, Female Officer in the French Army.—Christian Davies, *alias* Mother Ross.—Female Soldier in the 20th Foot.—Women of Barcelona.—Hannah Snell, Private in the Line and Marines.—Phœbe Hessel, Private in the 5th Regiment.—Paul Daniel, a Female Recruit.—Hannah Whitney and Anne Chamberlayne, Female Sailors.—Mary Ralphson.—"Pretty Polly Oliver."—Miss Jenny Cameron.—Anne Sophia Detzliffin, Prussian Female Soldier.—Madame de Drucourt (Siege of Louisburg).—Madame Ducharmy (Capture of Guadeloupe).—Chevalier d'Eon.—Deborah Samson, Private, and Molly Macaulay, Sergeant in the American Revolutionary Army.—Elizabeth Canning.—Catherine the Second of Russia and the Princess Daschkova.—Doña Rafaela Mora, Female Captain in the Spanish American Service (How Nelson Lost an Eye.)—Female Sailor on Board Admiral Rodney's Ship.

DURING the eighteenth century there were to be found in nearly every European army, one or more female soldiers. They sometimes held commissions as officers, but more frequently served as non-commissioned

officers or privates. Those women and girls who enlisted in the British Army were generally wives or sweethearts of soldiers whose regiments had been ordered abroad, and the women, preferring to encounter the dangers and hardships of a foreign campaign rather than the miseries of separation, disguised themselves in male attire and enlisted in some battalion which was embarking for the seat of war. Sometimes, indeed, women, deserted by their husbands, resolved to follow their unfaithful spouses all over the world: and, unable to afford travelling expenses, enlisted at the first recruiting depôt, and trusted to chance for meeting with or hearing of the object of their search. As no personal examination of recruits took place in those days, either in Great Britain or elsewhere, there was no way of finding out the imposture until afterwards, more especially as the female soldiers behaved themselves quite as *manly* as their comrades.

Of course in every country there have been local celebrities whose names even are unknown beyond the frontiers, for a man or woman must perform very great deeds to become famous in foreign lands. Thus it happens, while we are familiar with the names of many an English female soldier, we know of only two or three women who served during the last century in the armies of France. Yet the world well knows that Frenchwomen are second to none in warlike *esprit*. One of these Gallic warriors was Captain Bodeaux, an officer holding a commission as lieutenant in one of the regiments which went over to Ireland under the command of St. Ruth, to assist James the Second. This gallant officer distinguished herself at the battle of the Boyne, July 1st, 1690, where she met with Mr. Cavanaugh, father of Christian Davies. She stopped at the house of that gentleman (who was also fighting for King James) till about three in the morning, when, being alarmed, they fled together precipitately. Christian Davies describes this officer as " a very handsome young French gentleman," though the real sex of Bodeaux was not unknown to her. At the siege of Limerick, June, 1691, she held Thomond bridge, over the Shannon, with a small body of troops, against the English, till at last she fell, covered with wounds. Such was the bravery of this young French officer that her death was lamented even by the foe. Great was their astonishment when they found their valiant antagonist was a woman.

The most famous woman who has ever served as a private in any modern European army, was Christian (or Christiana) Davies, *alias* Mother Ross. She was born in 1667, in Dublin, " of parents whose probity acquired them that respect from their acquaintance which they had no claim to from their birth." Her father, Mr. Cavanaugh, was a brewer and maltster, employing upwards of twenty servants, exclusive of those engaged on his farm at Leslipp, where his wife and daughter resided. Christiana never liked sedentary work, and in the matter of education never made much progress. She had barely sufficient patience to learn reading, and to become a good needle-woman. Open air exercises were her delight; ploughing, hay-making, using the flail, and, above all, riding on horseback. "I used," she says, "to get astride upon the horses and ride them barebacked about the fields and ditches, by which I once got a terrible fall and spoiled a gray mare given to my brother by our grandfather." Mr. Cavanaugh never discovered the offender; but, to purchase the silence of a cowherd who saw her and the mare fall into a dry ditch, she was obliged, for a long time, to give him a cup of ale every night.

In 1685, when the Irish were arming for King James, Mr. Cavanaugh sold his corn and equipped a troop of horse, with which he joined that monarch. After enduring great hardships he was dangerously wounded at the battle of Aughrim, June 12th, 1691, and died a few days after. His property was confiscated by Government.

Previous to this, shortly after the departure of Mr. Cavanaugh from home, the Roman Catholic inhabitants of Leslipp blocked up the door of the parish church during divine service, with logs of wood, butchers' blocks, and any other heavy articles which came to hand. Christiana was at home when this occurred; but her mother being, with others, blockaded in the sacred edifice, she seized up a spit and ran to the rescue. Being resisted by a sergeant, she thrust the spit through his leg; then removing the things which blocked up the door, set the congregation free. Christiana was arrested for wounding the sergeant, but was afterwards liberated.

After the death of her father, Christian went on a visit to her aunt, the landlady of a public-house in Dublin, who, at her death, left the establishment to her niece. The latter married Richard Welsh, a good-looking young fellow who acted as barman and general assistant. After two boys had been born, her happiness was suddenly blighted by the mysterious disappearance of Richard, of whom nothing was heard for several months. At last, when she had given him up for dead, a letter arrived (the *twelfth* he had written) telling her how, on the day of his disappearance, he had been invited by an old friend on board a transport with recruits on board; the vessel set sail, and they had reached Helvoet Sluys before he could get ashore. Having no way of getting back to Ireland, he enlisted in a foot-regiment.

Christian resolved to follow her husband to Flanders. Letting the public-house, leaving her furniture with different friends, and placing one child with her grandmother and the other with a nurse, she dressed herself in a suit of her husband's clothes, cut her hair short, and went to the "Golden Last," where Ensign Laurence told the new recruit that she was "a clever, brisk young fellow," and enrolled her, under the name of Christopher Welsh, in the Marquis de Pisare's regiment of foot.

The recruits were disembarked at Williamstadt, in Holland. Thence they marched to Gorkhum, where they received their uniforms; and the next day they advanced to Landen, which they reached a day or two before the great battle of July 19th, 1693. Here they were incorporated into their respective battalions. Christian found the drill very easy, "having been accustomed," as she says, "to soldiers, when a girl, and delighted with seeing them exercise. I very soon was perfect," she adds, "and applauded by my officers for my dexterity in going through it."

The same night that she arrived at Landen, being on night-guard at the door of the Elector of Hanover (afterwards George I.), Christian was wounded by a musket-ball which grazed her leg, barely missing the bone. She was thus laid up for two months.

During the summer of 1694, Christian being out

with a foraging party, was made prisoner, and brought, together with three-score English and Dutch, to St. Germain-en-Laye. When the ex-Queen of England heard that Christian and her companions were English soldiers, she ordered that each man should have a pound of bread, a pint of wine, and five farthings each per diem, with clean straw every night. But the Dutch prisoners were not allowed these luxuries. The Duke of Berwick, a Marshal of France, visited the prison, and tried to persuade the British to follow his example and enter the service of the Grand Monarque. The chief annoyance which Christian suffered was the fear of being recognised by her cousin, Captain Cavanaugh, a French officer, who visited the prison nearly every day.

About nine days later, the English prisoners were exchanged, and on being set free they waited upon the Queen to thank her for her kindness. Her regiment passed the winter of 1694-5 in Gorkhum, where Christian passed her time "very merrily" by making love to the young and pretty daughter of a wealthy burgher. After a few weeks' courtship "the poor girl grew absolutely fond" of her military wooer. This *harmless frolic* led to a duel betwen Private Welsh and a sergeant of the regiment who wished to engage the girl's affections. Having dangerously wounded the sergeant, Christian was ordered under arrest; but the old father, who was in ignorance of the real state of the case, exerted his influence with the authorities, and procured her discharge from the regiment.

Bidding farewell to the girl, under pretence of going to purchase a commission, Christian enlisted in the 6th Dragoons, commanded by Lord John Hayes, and served all through the campaign of 1695, including the siege of Namur. Nothing remarkable happened to her till the Peace of Ryswick, Sept. 20th, 1697, when she was discharged, and went home to Ireland. None of her friends recognised the stalwart dragoon as being identical with Mrs Welsh; so, in place of claiming her property she found other means of support, until the War of the Spanish Succession broke out, in 1701. Returning to Holland, Christian re-enlisted in the 6th Dragoons.

She served through the campaigns of 1701-2, under the Duke of Marlborough, without being wounded. She was one of the captors of Venlo, Sept. 23rd, 1702, which proved a profitable investment for the English, for they found more than thirty pieces of cannon, twenty thousand florins, and a quantity of plate and jewellery. Christian complains that, the Grenadiers having the start of the Dragoons, she "got very little of the plunder." "I got, however," she confesses, "a large silver chalice and some other pieces of plate," which prize was sufficient to console her.

The Dragoons wintered at Venlo, and a night or two after their arrival she was ordered, with others, to escort the Duke of Marlborough along the banks of the Meuse. "During our march," says Christian, "by the darkness of the night we mistook our way, and going up the country fell in with a hogstye where was a sow with five pigs, one of which I made bold with. I was possessed of it some time," she adds, "when one Taylor, a corporal belonging to Brigadier Panton's Regiment of Horse, attempted to spoil me of my booty, whereupon some words arising, he drew, and made a stroke at my head, which I warding with my hand, had the sinew of my little finger cut in two; at the same time, with the butt-end of my pistol I struck out one of his eyes." Pretty discipline for British soldiers!

After serving all through the campaign of 1703, including the battle of Eckeren, and the sieges of Bonn and Lembourg, she was wounded in the hip at the battle of Donawert, July 2nd, 1704. The musket-ball lodged so firmly in the bone that the efforts of three surgeons in the hospital near Schellenberg were insufficient to extract it. Christian with difficulty warded off the discovery of her sex.

She left hospital just in time to assist in plundering the Bavarians. "We spared nothing," says she; "burning or otherwise destroying whatever we could not carry off. The bells of the churches we broke to pieces that we might bring them away with us. I filled three bed-ticks, after having emptied them of the feathers, with bell-metal, men's and women's clothes, some velvets, and about one hundred Dutch caps which I had plundered from a shop." Besides these things she got several pieces of plate, as spoons, mugs, cups, etc.

After the battle of Blenheim, August 2nd, 1704, in which she was in the midst of the fight, under the hottest of the fire, Christian was appointed one of the guard despatched with the prisoners to Breda. Having halted to refresh themselves with a pint of beer and a pennyworth of bread each (the prisoners being allowed the same indulgence), Christian saw the long-lost Richard Welsh, now a sergeant in the Earl of Orkney's regiment of foot, making love to a Dutch woman. She abused him heartily at first, but she soon forgave him. It was agreed that she should remain in the army and pass as his brother. On her return to her regiment she assisted in the siege of Landau. Nothing of any consequence happened to her during the campaign of 1705.

On the 23rd of May, 1706, was fought the great battle of Ramilies. When the French were retreating, Christian, who had fought valiantly during the engagement, was struck in the head by " an unlucky shell " fired from a mortar planted on the steeple of the church. Her skull was fractured, and she was carried to the hospital of Meldré or Meldret, where her head was trepanned. During a ten weeks' illness the long-dreaded discovery of her sex was made. The surgeons sent word to Brigadier Preston that his " pretty Dragoon " was a woman. The Brigadier, who would at first scarcely believe the news, told Christian that he had always looked upon her " as the prettiest fellow, and the best man he had." The story soon spread through the regiment, and Christian was visited by Lord John Hayes and all her officers and comrades. Lord John gave strict orders that she should want for nothing, and promised that her pay as a dragoon should be continued till she had quitted the hospital.

Of course she could no longer stop in the regiment. " Brigadier Preston " she says " made me a present of a handsome silk gown; every one of the officers contributed to furnishing me with whatever was requisite for the dress of my sex, and dismissed me the service with a handsome compliment." Her husband having been questioned relative to their previous acquaintance, it was thought prudent to have them married again; and this second wedding was celebrated with much solemnity, in presence of all the officers, " who, everyone, at taking leave, would kiss the bride, and left me," adds Christian, "a piece of gold, some four or five, to put me in a way of life."

For a short time she carried on the business of cook to the 6th Dragoons; but finding the work too heavy, she turned sutler, and was permitted, as a special favour, to pitch her tent in the front of the army, the other sutlers being driven to the rear. She spent much time in marauding; and one day in 1708, being in male garb, she and her mule were taken prisoner. However, she persuaded the French officer to let her go. Shortly before this she hired herself as cook to the head sutler of the British army, Mr. Dupper, who afterwards kept a tavern on Fish Street Hill, London.

Richard Welsh was slain at the siege of Mons, in September, 1709. Her grief, she tells us, was something terrible. It was on this occasion that she first came to be styled Mother Ross. "Captain Ross came by, who seeing my agony, could not forbear sympathizing with me and dropped some tears, protesting that the poor woman's grief touched him nearer than the loss of so many brave men. This confession from the Captain gave me the nick-name of Mother Ross, by which I became better known than by that of my husband."

Eleven weeks after the death of Welsh, his sorrowing widow was persuaded to bestow her hand on Hugh Jones, Grenadier, who was killed at the siege of St. Venant, 1710. During this and the following year Christian held the post of under-cook in Lord Stair's kitchen.

On the close of the campaign of 1712 she returned to England, and called on the Duke of Marlborough; but he, being in disgrace, advised her to wait on the Duke of Argyle. The latter told Christian to draw up a petition to the Queen. Her majesty received Mother Ross very graciously, and gave her an order on the Earl of Oxford for fifty pounds. But having waited on the Earl several times and seen neither him nor the money, she petitioned the Queen again. Anne granted a second order for the same sum, payable this time on Sir William Windham, and Christian was also put on the pension list for a shilling a day. Sir William at once paid the fifty pounds; but the Earl of Oxford, without speaking to Queen Anne, cut down the pension to five-pence. On the accession of George I., she succeeded in having it raised again to a shilling; and this pension she retained till her death.

Immediately after receiving the money, Christian returned to Dublin; but being unable to recover either her house or furniture, she set up a beershop. She was keeping herself very comfortably, "till my evil genius," she laments, "entangled me in a third marriage." This time the bridegroom was named Davies, and belonged to the Welsh Fusileers. His regiment was ordered, soon after the marriage, to England; Christian therefore sold her effects, and returned to London, where she established a shop in Willow Walk, Tothill Fields, Westminster, for the sale of strong liquors and farthing pies. This was in 1715. She prospered so well, that after the return of her husband from Preston (where he had gone to fight the Pretender), she was able to purchase his discharge; but "in two days after his arrival in London, being drunk, he enlisted in the Guards." During the November of this year, Mother Ross kept a sutler's tent in Hyde Park where the Life and Foot Guards were encamped.

Her husband was a constant source of trouble and vexation. Some friends having obtained his discharge, he spent her money so fast that she was obliged to give up, successively, public-houses at Paddington and in Charles-street, Westminster. She returned to Dublin, when the Lord-Lieutenant granted her the exclusive privilege of selling beer in the Phœnix Park on review-days. Tiring of this, in less than a year, she returned to England; and after living three years in Chester, she entered Chelsea College as a Pensioner. She also succeeded in obtaining a sergeantcy in the College for her husband. Here she resided till her death: being supported by the benevolence of several members of the nobility—principally officers who had known her as Mother Ross. She went to Court twice a-week to keep herself in the minds of her patrons; "but," she laments, "the expense of coach-hire, as both my lameness and age increases, for I cannot walk ten yards without help, is a terrible tax upon their charity, and at the same time many of my old friends no longer going to Court, my former subsistence is greatly diminished from what it was."

For some months previous to her death Christian Davies's health was undermined by dropsy, scurvy, and other disorders. But the chief cause of her last illness was sitting up several nights by the bedside of her husband. This brought on a severe cold, which threw her into a fever, of which she died, July 7th, 1739. She was interred with military honours in the burial-ground of Chelsea College, Her autobiography, edited by Daniel Defoe, was published in 1740. A second edition came out in 1741, with a vignette frontispiece representing Christian Davies first in her Dragoon's uniform, and then in the dress of a sutler.

According to the embarkation returns of the 20th Foot, dated 1st July, 1702, preserved among the Harleian MSS. at the British Museum, one of the soldiers in Captain St. Clair's Company was found to be a woman. The regiment was embarking to join the expedition against Cadiz.

During the war of the Spanish Succession, Catalonia having declared against Philip, the French claimant to the crown, was invaded and ravaged by the forces of Louis Quatorze. Barcelona, the capital, was invested for several months, and the formidable artillery of France played, almost unceasingly, on the walls. But the people, nothing daunted by the arrival of Marshal Berwick with twenty thousand men to reinforce the besiegers, made a most resolute defence. All who could bear arms flew to aid in the defence; the priests and the women enrolled themselves in the ranks, and fought with the same desperate valour as the rest. Their courage, however, was unavailing; for the city was taken by assault, Sept. 11th, 1714.

Hannah Snell, another British heroine, was born in Fryer-street, Winchester, on the 23rd of April, 1723. Military predilections ran in the family; her grandfather served under King William and the Duke of Marlborough, and was slain in the battle of Malplaquet. Her father, however, was a simple dyer and hosier. Hannah was the youngest but one of a family of three sons and six daughters.

On the death of her father and mother in 1740,

Hannah came to London, and lived for some time in Ship-street, Wapping, in the house of one of her sisters, Mrs. Gray, whose husband was a carpenter. She had not resided in the house very long before she became acquainted with James Summs, a Dutch sailor, whom she married, Jan. 6th, 1743, after a courtship of about two years. Her marriage was not a happy one. After squandering the little property belonging to his wife, spending it in the lowest debauchery, James became heavily involved in debt, and deserted her altogether. Hannah, left without the means of support, was obliged to return to the house of her sister, where, two months after, her child, a girl, was born.

Notwithstanding his vile conduct, Mrs. Summs still dearly loved her husband; and on the death of her child, she resolved to set out in search of the truant. Dressing herself in a suit of clothes belonging to her brother-in-law, which, together with his name, she borrowed, Hannah left London, Nov. 23rd, 1743, and reached Coventry without hearing any news of her missing husband. On the 27th of the same month she enlisted, under the name of James Gray, in General Guise's regiment of Foot (the 6th, or Royal First Warwickshire). After remaining about three weeks in the town, during which she made numberless inquiries about James

Summs, Hannah was sent with seventeen comrades to join her regiment at Carlisle.

She was soon very proficient in the drill; but at the same time she had the misfortune to incur the enmity of Davis, a sergeant in her company, who wished to employ the new recruit in a somewhat dishonourable affair with a girl who lived in Carlisle. Hannah, however, disclosed the real intentions of the sergeant to the intended victim, and gained the love of the girl, while she made a bitter enemy of Davis. The latter, from seeing Hannah and the other very frequently together, grew terribly jealous; he seized the first opportunity to charge his supposed rival with neglect of duty. Hannah was sentenced to receive six hundred lashes. After five hundred had been administered, the officers interceded, and obtained for her the remission of the other hundred.

The tyranny of Davis soon became unbearable; and, to make matters worse, a carpenter from Worcester, who had lodged in the house of Hannah's brother-in-law, enlisted in the regiment, and she was in constant terror lest he should recognise and betray her. To get away without the discovery of her sex was now the great object of her thoughts. She borrowed a small sum of money from the girl in Carlisle, deserted, and set off on foot for Portsmouth. About a mile from Carlisle she saw several men and women picking peas; their clothes lay about, at a short distance, and Hannah very speedily exchanged her soldier's coat for an old jacket.

At Liverpool she entered a small public-house; and, by affecting to make love to the landlady, made the landlord so jealous that a match of "fisticuffs" ensued. Boniface, however, got the worst of it, and was compelled to keep his bed all next day. Hannah borrowed some money of the landlady, and made the best of her way to Chester, where she took genteel lodgings in a private house.

It chanced that a pretty young mantua-maker lodged in the same house. Hannah contrived to make the acquaintance of the girl, and speedily won her heart, together with five guineas. The handsome young suitor levanted to Winchester, where, in an attempt on the heart of a widow, she met her match. She speedily quitted the town, with only a few shillings in her pocket.

In about a month from the day she left Carlisle, Hannah reached Portsmouth, where she enlisted in Colonel Fraser's Regiment of Marines. With others of her regiment, she embarked, three weeks later, for the East Indies. The "Swallow" formed part of Admiral Boscawen's fleet. Hannah soon earned the praises of the officers for her dexterity in washing, mending, and cooking. Mr. Wyegate, Lieutenant of Marines, was so greatly interested in the young private, that he invited her to become one at the officers' mess.

The "Swallow" suffered from some terrible storms, which destroyed almost all her rigging, and reduced the vessel almost to the condition of a wreck. It was refitted at Gibraltar; proceeding thence by the Cape of Good Hope to the Mauritius, which Admiral Boscawen unsuccessfully attacked. Thence the fleet sailed to Fort St. David on the Coromandel coast; where the marines being disbanded, joined the British force encamped before Areacoping. The place surrendered after a siege of ten days. During the siege Hannah displayed so much courage that she received the commendations of all her officers.

The British next laid siege to Pondicherry; but after suffering terrible hardships, they were forced by the rainy season to raise the siege in eleven weeks. Hannah was one of the first body of British soldiers who forded the river, breast high, under an incessant fire from the French batteries. She was also for seven nights successively on duty in the picket-ground, and worked exceedingly hard for upwards of fourteen days in the trenches.

She was dangerously wounded in one of the attacks. During this action she fired thirty-seven rounds, and received in return six shots in her right leg, five in the left leg, and a dangerous wound in the abdomen; the last-named being excessively painful. She was terrified lest these wounds would lead to the discovery of her sex; so in place of letting the army-surgeons dress all her wounds, she kept silence about the most dangerous of them, though it was at the risk of her life. Entrusting the secret to no one but a black woman who waited on her, Hannah extracted the bullet with her finger and thumb; the negress obtained lint, salve, and other necessaries for dressing, and the wound was soon perfectly cured.

Hannah was removed for the cure of her other wounds to the hospital at Cuddalore; and before her recovery, the greater part of the fleet had sailed. She was sent on board the " Tartar Pink," and performed all the regular duties of a sailor, till the return of the fleet from Madras, when she was turned over to the " Eltham " man-of-war. On board this ship she sailed to Bombay. The vessel sprang a leak, and they were obliged to stop here five weeks to repair.

One night the Lieutenant of the "Eltham," who commanded in the absence of Captain Lloyd, wishing to pass the time agreeably, asked Hannah for a song. She declined, on the plea of being unwell; but the officer would take no denial. Hannah became obstinate, but soon she had cause to regret her folly. Shortly after, she was accused of stealing a shirt belonging to one of her comrades. The Lieutenant, having a grudge against Hannah, ordered her to be put in irons; and after five days' confinement, ordered her to the gangway, where she received five lashes. The shirt was afterwards found in the box of the very man who had complained of losing it.

Returning to Fort St. David, the "Eltham" rejoined the squadron, which departed soon after on its homeward voyage. Hannah was terribly "chaffed" during the voyage because she had no beard; and she became known among the sailors by the name of Miss Molly Gray. But in place of resenting this, Hannah, to show she was as good a man as any of them, plunged headlong into all the amusements and enjoyments of the others, and they soon forgot the old nickname, for which they substituted that of "Hearty Jemmy."

One night, in a house of entertainment at Lisbon, she learned, from an English sailor who had been in a Dutch ship at Genoa, that James Summs, her husband, was dead. He had murdered a gentleman of high position in Genoa, and for this crime he was put into a bag full of stones, and flung into the sea.

The British fleet arrived at Spithead in 1750. Hannah left the "Eltham," and came to London, where she was cordially welcomed by her sister. The strange story of Hannah Snell soon became generally known; and as she had a good voice, the managers of the Royalty Theatre, Wellclose Square, engaged her to appear before the footlights as Bill Bobstay, Firelock, and other military and naval heroes, and to go through the manual and platoon exercises with a musket. But she did not long remain on the stage, as, in consideration of the wounds she received during the siege of Pondicherry, she was put on the out-pensioners' list at Chelsea Hospital. Her pension was increased by a special grant to twenty pounds a year, and paid regularly to the day of her death. With the assistance of some friends she set up a public-house at Wapping, by which she realized a very good income. On one side of the sign-board there was painted the figure of a jovial British tar, on the other a portrait of herself in her marine's uniform. Underneath the last was inscribed, " The Widow in Masquerade, or the Female Warrior."

Hannah preferred masculine attire, and continued to wear men's clothes for the rest of her life. She lived long to enjoy her prosperity; but during the latter years of her life she became a lunatic, and died, at the age of sixty-nine, in Bedlam.

Phœbe Hessel (or Hassel) was for many years a private in the 5th Regiment, and served under the Duke of Cumberland in many engagements, amongst others the battle of Fontenoy. The fatigues and hardships of war certainly did not tend to shorten her days. Born during the reign of Queen Anne, she lived to see the accession of George IV. Indeed, it was through the liberality of the last-named monarch that Phœbe was enabled to live comfortably during the latter years of her life. When the Prince Regent visited Brighton, he saw old Phœbe, who was living there, maintained by some of the more benevolent inhabitants. Having heard her strange story, the Prince told some one to ask her what sum she required to make her comfortable.

"Half-a-guinea a week," replied Phœbe, "will make me as happy as a princess."

This annuity was, by order of the Prince Regent, paid to her as long as she lived.

Phœbe Hessel was a woman of good information, and very communicative. Her stories were always worth hearing. She retained all her faculties till within a few hours of her death, which took place Dec. 12th, 1821. She was buried in Brighton Churchyard, and a tombstone erected over her grave by public subscription. The following inscription was carved thereon :—

" Sacred to the memory of Phœbe Hessel, born Sept. 1st, 1713. She served for many years as a private soldier in the 5th regiment, in different parts of Europe, and in 1745 fought under the Duke of Cumberland in the battle of Fontenoy, where she received a bayonet wound in the arm ; her long life which commenced in the reign of queen Anne, induced his present Majesty George IV. to grant her a pension. She died at Brighton, where she had long resided, Dec. 12th, 1821, aged 108 years.

In August, 1761, as a sergeant was exercising some recruits on board a transport at Portsmouth, he noticed that one of them, who had enlisted under the name of Paul Daniel, had a more prominent breast than the others. When the firing was over, the sergeant sent for Daniel to the cabin, and told him his suspicion that he was a woman. After some evasions the recruit confessed her sex; and said that she had a husband, to whom she was devotedly attached, who, after squandering a plentiful fortune, had reduced himself and her to beggary, and had then enlisted. His regiment had been ordered to Germany in 1759 to serve against the French, and had remained abroad ever since. Not having heard from him for two years, she had resolved to roam the world in search of him. She heard that the British Government were sending more troops to Germany, so she enlisted in one of the regiments ordered thither, thinking to meet her husband. When the discovery of her sex frustrated this design, she declared herself to be inconsolable.

In October of the same year, a young woman aged

about twenty, attired in nautical garb, was seized at Plymouth by the Press-gang, and sent to Captain Toby. On her capture she was placed for safety in the town jail. Not relishing her imprisonment, she roundly abused Captain Toby, told him she was a woman, that her name was Hannah Whitney, that she was born in Ireland, and had served on board several British men-of-war for upwards of five years. She concluded by informing the astounded captain that she would never have discovered her sex if they had not placed her in a common jail. Of course she was immediately released.

There is (or was) a monument in Chelsea church, commemorative of the masculine courage of Anne Chamberlayne, only daughter of Edward Chamberlayne, Doctor of Laws. She appears to have been infected with an ardour for naval glory by her two brothers, who were both distinguished officers on board men-of-war. Putting on the dress of a sailor, she joined the crew of a fine ship, commanded by one of her brothers; and in an engagement with the French, she fought most gallantly for upwards of six hours.

On the 27th of June, 1808, died at Liverpool Mary Ralphson, a Scottish heroine. She was born in Lochaber, June 1st, 1698; and married Ralph

Ralphson, then a private in the British army. She followed her husband in all his campaigns under the Duke of Cumberland, and was present with him in several famous engagements. On the breaking out of the war in French Flanders she embarked with the troops, and shared their toils and vicissitudes. Being present on the field of Dettingen during the heat of the conflict, surrounded with heaps of the slain, she saw a wounded dragoon fall dead by her side. She disguised herself in his clothes, and regained the British camp; then returned with her husband to England. After this she accompanied him in his later campaigns under the Duke of Cumberland. She lived to a fine old age, and was supported during her declining years chiefly by some benevolent ladies of Liverpool.

There is just a hint of a loyal Jacobite heroine in a curious old Scotch ballad called "Polly Oliver's Ramble." The song commences:—

> "As pretty Polly Oliver lay musing in bed,
> A comical fancy came into her head;
> Nor father nor mother shall make me false prove,
> I'll list for a soldier and follow my love."

There is an old song on the Pretender which appears to be a parody on this ballad. This begins:—

> "As Perkin one morning lay musing in bed,
> The thought of three kingdoms ran much in his head."

In June, 1745, Charles Edward Stuart, the young Pretender, landed in Scotland to assert his father's right to the British crown. He was joined by most of the Highland chieftains with their clans, and he sent to all those lairds who had not yet paid their allegiance, to do so without delay. Lochiel, his lieutenant, wrote to Cameron, the Laird of Glendessary, commanding him to appear at headquarters immediately, with as many of his clan, armed, as he could muster in so short a notice.

The laird was a minor, and, moreover, a youth of little capacity; so his aunt, Miss Jenny Cameron, roused the clan to arms, and marched, at the head of two hundred and fifty claymores, to the camp of Bonnie Prince Charlie. She rode into camp on a bay gelding decked out in green trappings, trimmed with gold. She wore a sea-green riding habit with scarlet lappets edged with gold. Her hair was tied behind in loose buckles, and covered by a velvet cap with scarlet feathers. In her hand, in lieu of a whip, she carried a drawn sword.

A female soldier was a sight not to be seen every day. The Prince immediately quitted the lines to receive her. Miss Jenny rode up to him without the slightest embarrassment; and giving the military salute, told him "as her nephew was not able to attend the royal standard, she had raised men, and now brought them to his highness; that she believed them ready to hazard their lives in his cause; and that, although at present they were commanded by a woman, yet she hoped they had nothing womanish about them; for she found that so glorious a cause had raised in her own heart every manly thought and quite extinguished the woman. What effect then must it have on those who have no feminine fear to combat, and are free from the incumbrance of female dress. These men," she added, "are yours; they have devoted themselves to your service, they bring you hearts as well as hands. I can follow them no farther," she said, "but I shall pray for your success."

The clansmen then passed in review before the prince. When this was over, he conducted Miss Cameron to his tent, where she was entertained with the utmost courtesy and hospitality. Prince Charlie gave her the title of "Colonel Cameron," and by this epithet she was distinguished for many years.

Miss Jenny remained with the Jacobite army until it invaded England, and joined it again on its return, in Annandale. She was still in camp in January, 1746, and fought in the battle of Falkirk on the 23rd; when she was made prisoner, and lodged in Edinburgh Castle. She was ultimately set at liberty, and returned to the guardianship of her weak-minded nephew.

A Highland song was composed in her honour, relating how :

> "Miss Jenny Cameron,
> She put her belt and hanger on,
> And away to the Young Pretender."

Anne Sophia Detzliffin, who served four years in the Prussian army, was born in 1738 at Treptow on the Rega. In 1757, during the Seven Years' War, she was excited by a thirst for glory to quit her father's house and go to Colberg, where she enlisted in Prince Frederic's regiment of cuirassiers. She remained in this corps for two years, and fought in several actions; in one of which, near Bamberg, she received a sabre-wound in her left arm.

She next fought in the battle of Kunnersdorff. Her regiment returned some days later to Saxony, where Anne fell dangerously ill, and was sent to the hospital of Meissen. She soon recovered, but having no opportunity for rejoining her regiment, she enlisted in a battalion of Grenadiers, which was decimated shortly after in the actions of Strechlin and Torgau, in 1760. In the latter, fought on Nov. 3rd, Sophia Detzliffin received two severe wounds on the head, and was captured by the Austrians, who took her to the hospital at Dresden.

When she had almost recovered, the heroine found means to escape from the hospital. Passing through the Austrian outposts without being discovered, she enlisted (in 1761) with Colonel Colignon, who sent her to a regiment of Le Noble's Volunteers.

After serving in this corps for two months, she was accused on the 14th of July by one of her comrades of robbing him of fourteen-pence. There was not the slightest foundation for the accusation; but a subaltern immediately placed her under arrest. Anne was determined not to submit to such an indignity. Sending for her lieutenant, she told that she was a female, and declared that during four years' service in various regiments she had never once been ordered under arrest, nor even received a blow for neglect of duty. She concluded by telling the officer that after this insult she would no longer remain in the army—which was, however, a needless remark, as she would not have been permitted to stop after her sex was known.

This heroine, when she quitted the army, was twenty-three years old, with strongly-marked features, and a brown complexion.

On the 8th of June, 1758, General (afterwards Lord) Amherst, with an army of twelve thousand men, in which General Wolfe served as a brigadier, landed on the island of Cape-Breton, in Canada, and commenced the siege of Louisbourg. This town was so strongly fortified that the French, believing it to be impregnable, left only two thousand eight hundred men for its defence. The military commander, the Chevalier de Drucourt, was a brave and resolute soldier, and made a gallant defence. The British, however, determined to make up for all their recent disasters, commenced the siege with more than ordinary vigour and energy. The Chevalier was ably assisted in the defence by his wife; who, appearing on the walls among the common soldiers, exhorted them to fight bravely in defence of the town. And not only did she thus cheer them by encouraging words; she carried round food and ammunition to the exhausted soldiers, and occasionally took her turn at the guns, which she loaded and fired with skill and rapidity. But the efforts of the Chevalier and his wife were of no avail against the superior numbers of the English. Louisbourg surrendered on the 26th of June; and the Chevalier and Madame de Drucourt were made prisoners. However, General Amherst treated his brave captives with the greatest respect and hospitality.

In 1759, when the British were besieging Guadaloupe, the native planters were incited to resist the invaders by M. Dutril, the French Governor. Amongst others, Madame Ducharmy, wife of a planter, armed her servants and negroes, and led them to an attack on the British forces.

Amongst the celebrities of the eighteenth century, none was more famous than the Chevalier d'Eon. Even before the strange question as to his real sex had been raised, the Chevalier was well known in every European court as a skilful diplomatist and a brave soldier. In 1761, having attained the summit of his glory in the political world, he sighed for military renown. As aide-de-camp to Marshal Broglio, he distinguished himself most highly against the British and Prussians. Being entrusted with the removal of the military stores from Hoxter, which the French were evacuating, he passed the Weser with several boats, under a heavy fire from the enemy, and saved all the baggage. Shortly after this he was wounded in the head and thigh in a skirmish at Ultrop.

On the 7th September, at the head of the Grenadiers de Champagne and the Swiss Guards, the Chevalier attacked a Highland regiment ("Montagnards Ecossais," Broglio styles them in his despatch) near the village of Meinsloff, and after a slight skirmish, drove them back to the British camp. At Osterwick, with about fifty dragoons and hussars, D'Eon charged a Prussian battalion six or seven hundred strong, which was intercepting the communications of the French with Wolfembutel. The Prussians, seized with a panic, threw down their arms, and surrendered. The capture of Wolfembutel by Marshal Saxe was the result of this brilliant action.

The preliminaries of peace in September, 1762, terminated the Chevalier's military career, and he returned to the political world, where he had already made himself so distinguished. He was sent to London, as Secretary of Legation under the Duc de Nivernois, the Ambassador-Extraordinary. On the return of the Duc to Paris, the Chevalier remained in London first as resident, and afterwards as minister plenipotentiary at the Court of St. James's. At this period his star was at its zenith. Fortune lavished her favours upon him with the most profuse liberality. Suddenly the wheel turned; and, without any reason being assigned, D'Eon was dismissed from all his appointments, and compelled to reside, disgraced, in London. The French ministers who had negotiated the peace now effected his ruin. The treaty had been considered disgraceful to France, both by the king and the people; and the negotiators, afraid of the Chevalier, who knew too much, found means to disgrace him. Louis XV., however, settled upon D'Eon a pension of twelve hundred livres.

During the Chevalier's residence in London, suspicions arose in the minds of several persons that D'Eon was a disguised woman. The notion soon reached the Continent; and both in England and abroad, some very extraordinary wagers were made on the subject. In July, 1777, a trial took place before Lord Chief Justice Mansfield on an action brought by a Mr. Hayes against a Mr. Jacques, the latter of whom had received several premiums of fifteen guineas, to return one hundred whenever it should be proved, beyond a doubt, that the Chevalier D'Eon was a woman. MM. Louis Legoux and de Morande deposed to this as a fact so thoroughly established, that the defendant's counsel actually pleaded that the wager was unfair, because the plaintiff knew, before it was laid, that the Court of France had treated with the Chevalier as a woman. The plaintiff, however, obtained a verdict, which was afterwards set aside on the ground of the bet being illegal.

Shortly after the conclusion of the trial, the Chevalier d'Eon, for some unaccountable reason, put on female attire, which he contrived to wear until his death.

Everybody now believed that D'Eon was a woman. Several portraits were published representing him in various characters—as an officer of dragoons, as a French minister, as a fashionable lady, etc. Mr. Hooper, of Ludgate-hill, published a mezzotinto engraving of the Chevalier as Pallas, a casque on her head, a lance in her right hand, and the ægis on her left arm. Round the edge of the shield were the words *At nunc dura dedit vobis discrimina Pallas.* On each side were drums, muskets, pyramids of cannon-balls, heavy pieces of ordnance, and a pair of colours on which were written, *Impavidam serient ruinæ*. In the middle distance might be seen a citadel and a camp. The lower part of the engraving contained representations of the principal events of the Chevalier's life, with a eulogy, in English, on his talents and virtues. After rapturously praising the genius, the courage, the personal beauty of D Eon, this eulogy concludes by saying that " her military comrades offer this homage as an eternal monument of their affection."

The breaking out of the French Revolution deprived D'Eon of his pension. He returned to France in 1792 and offered his services to the National Assembly. But they were declined; and on his return to England his name was placed on the list of Emigrants. He was now plunged into the depths of poverty, and supported himself as best he could by giving lessons in fencing. But he depended chiefly on the kindness of Elisée, first surgeon to Louis XVIII., and other friends. He died May the 21st, 1810, when Elisèe assisted in the dissection of his body; and declared that the Chevalier belonged to the male sex.

During the American War of Independence

several women donned masculine attire and enlisted in the Revolutionary Army. One of these heroines was named Deborah Samson. Born at Plymouth, U.S., of very poor parents, she was received at an early age into a respectable family, where the members treated her with great kindness. Her education was at first totally neglected, though she remedied this, to the best of her ability, by teaching herself to read and write; later in life she saved enough to pay for her schooling. In 1778, having dressed herself in male attire, she enlisted under the name of Robert Shirtliffe for the whole term of the war.

Deborah was used to all kinds of hardships, so the fatigues incident to her new life had as little effect on her as on her comrades. Her courage and obedience to military discipline, soon gained for her the esteem of the officers. She served as a volunteer in several expeditions, where her regiment was not engaged, and received two severe wounds—one in the head, the other in the shoulder. She managed, however, to avoid the disclosure of her sex.

At last Deborah Samson was seized with a brain fever in Philadelphia. The physician who attended her made the dreaded discovery, and sent word to the colonel of her regiment. When her health was restored, the colonel sent her with a letter to General Washington. Deborah saw that the truth was known, and it was with great reluctance she obeyed. Washington read the missive, without speaking a word. When he had finished, he handed Deborah Samson a discharge in which was enclosed some money and a letter containing good advice.

Some years after her discharge Deborah married Benjamin Garnett, of Sharon, Massachusetts. For her services as a revolutionary soldier, she was presented with a grant of land and a pension for life.

Another American heroine was Molly Macauley, a Pennsylvanian woman, who rose to the rank of sergeant in the national army, and fought bravely in several battles and skirmishes. Nobody suspected that she was other than she seemed to be—a brave, enthusiastic young American patriot. She was tall and stout, rough-looking, with all the manners of a soldier. In the enthusiasm of the moment she would swing her sabre over her head, and hurrah for "Mad Anthony," as General Wayne was styled.

She was wounded at Brandywine, and her sex discovered. She then returned home.

Another woman, whose name was long remembered in American homes, was Elizabeth Canning. She was at Fort Washington, her husband was slain, she took his place at a gun, loading, priming, and firing with good effect, till she was wounded in the breast by a grape shot.

Besides these examples, many women were frequently detected, disguised, in the American armies; and as they endured the same privations, with even less murmuring than the men, there was nothing, save accident, to reveal their sex. The instances are numerous of women and girls who aided in the defence of private houses. Their names, however, have very seldom reached Europe.

When Catherine the Second of Russia was conspiring to dethrone her husband, Peter III., she based her hopes of success almost entirely on the belief that the Imperial Guard would declare in her favour. On the 26th of June, 1762, she was seated in her palace at St. Petersburg, taking a slight repast in company with her early friend and confidant Catherine Romanowna, Princess of Daschkow, or Daschkova. The latter was born in 1744, a descendant of the noble family of Woronzoff, and became a widow at the early age of eighteen. She applied all her woman's wit to place Catherine on the throne. When their repast was concluded, Catherine proposed that they should ride at the head of their troops to Peterhoff; and to make themselves more popular with the soldiers, the Empress borrowed the uniform of Talitzen, a captain in the Preobraginsky Guards, while the Princess Daschkova donned the regimentals of Lieutenant Pouschkin, in which, she says, she looked "like a boy of fifteen."

It chanced by good luck that these uniforms were the same which had been worn from the time of Peter the Great until superseded by the Prussian uniform introduced by Peter III.

On the 29th July the Empress and her friend, still in uniform, passed in review twelve thousand soldiers, besides numberless volunteers. As Catherine rode along the ranks, amidst the cheers of the soldiers, a young ensign, observing that she had no tassel on her sword, untied his own and presented it. Thirty years afterwards, this man died a field-marshal and a Prince of the Russian Empire. His name was Potemkin.

It is said the Princess (though she makes no mention of it in her memoirs) requested, as the reward of her services, to be given the command of the Imperial Guard. The Empress refused; and the Princess, finding her inflexible, gave up her military aspirations and devoted herself to study. After her return from abroad in 1782, she was appointed Director of the Academy of Sciences, and President of the newly-established Russian Academy. She wrote much in her native tongue; amongst other works, several comedies. She died at Moscow in 1810.

It is a curious fact that no one has been able to say precisely when and where Nelson lost his left eye. Some say that the disaster occurred during the siege of Bastia, in 1793, while others decide that it was at the siege of Calvi. According to Signor D. Liberato Abarca, general in the service of the Nicaraguan Republic, both these accounts are false. He says that it was in the year 1780, when the future "god of the seas," then a post-captain in the royal navy, was cruising along the coast of Central America, that he received the wound which added him to the list of one-eyed warriors. After inflicting every possible injury on the Spanish colonies, Nelson resolved to take the Castle of San Carlos de Nicaragua by assault. He rowed up the river of San Juan, which flows into the Gulf of Mexico, with a flotilla of launches and other flat-bottomed boats. The Spanish commander was laid up in bed with a severe illness; and the garrison, terrified at the imposing preparations of the English sailors, hastily evacuated the fort. Doña Rafaela Mora, the wife or daughter of the commander, was left alone in the castle; and with great—what would at first sight appear to be reckless—daring resolved to drive the enemy from before the place. The guns were pointed towards the river, and nearly all loaded. Snatching up a burning match which the terrified soldiers had thrown down in their hasty retreat, Rafaela fired all the cannons one after another. One of the balls struck the boat in which Nelson stood; a splinter from the bulwark hit him in the face, just below left the eye. Such was the force of the blow, he was knocked down, and rendered perfectly insensible. This disaster broke up the siege, and the flotilla descended the stream with all speed.

The heroine received by royal decree the brevet of a captain on active service, together with a full suit of regimentals, which she was permitted to wear whenever she pleased. Besides this, a pension was settled upon her for the rest of her life. General Thomas Martinez, Director of the Republic of Nicaragua, is a descendant of Doña Rafaela Mora. General Abarca says the truth of this story is proved incontestably by documents which he has seen in the archives of the city of Granada, in Nicaragua.

During a sea-fight between the British and French fleets, Admiral Rodney observed a woman helping at one of the guns on the main deck of his ship. He asked her what brought her there?

"An't please your honour," said she, "my husband is sent down to the cock-pit wounded, and I am here to supply his place. Do you think, your honour," she added, " I am afraid of the *French?* "

After the battle was over, the Admiral sent for the woman, and told her that she had been guilty of a breach of discipline in being on board at all. However, he modified his rebuke by a gift of ten guineas·

II.

The Furies—Rose Lacombe—Théroigne de Méricourt—Madame Cochet—Marie Adrian (Siege of Lyons)—Renée Langerin—Madlle. de la Rochefoucault—Madame Dufief (War in La Vendée)—Felicité and Théophile de Fernig, Officers on Dumouriez's Staff—Mary Schelienck—Thérèse Figueur, French Dragoon—" William Roberts," the Manchester Heroine, Sergeant in the 15th Light Dragoons and the 37th Foot—Mary Anne Talbot, Drummer in the 82nd, Cabin Boy on board the Brunswick, and Middy on board the Vesuvius—Highland Soldier's Wife at the Storming of New Vigie—Susan Frost—Peggy Monro (Irish Rebellion)—Martha Glar and other Swiss Heroines—Queen of Prussia at Jena—Marie Anne Elise Bonaparte, Princess Bacciochi—Maid of Saragossa—Manuella Sanchez, Benita, and other Heroines of Saragossa—Spanish Female Captain—Mrs. Dalbiac (Battle of Salamanca)—Ellenora Prochaska, Private in Lutzow's Rifle Corps—Augusta Frederica Krüger, Prussian Soldier—Louise Belletz, French Artillery Soldier—Mrs. Heald and Mrs. Helm (Chicago Massacre).

THE Furies were the female warriors of the Reign of Terror. When we think of their ferocious bravery, their barbarous, maniacal cruelty, the ascendency which they held, even over the great Republican leaders, their wild cries and still wilder deeds, they seem more like the weird figures in some hideous German legend than real, living, sentient women, with human hearts. Women, indeed, they could scarcely be termed; Amazons they were, as brave and as cruel as those of the Euxine. Yet, fiends though they appeared, they had often the pangs of hunger to goad them on; and if cruelty such as theirs *can* be excused, starvation is the most reasonable plea that could be advanced.

Though many of the large towns possessed Furies in those days, Paris was their proper home. There they lived on the sight, the smell, the taste of human blood. To picture their history rightly, the pen should be dipped in blood. Blood, since they were denied bread was all they cared for; and when aristocratic heads grew scarce, these fiends turned on one another, like famished wolves, to glut their insatiable thirst. The Guillotine was a central rallying point for the Furies. Round it they danced and sang by day; its steps formed their pillow by night. There they crowded together—Tricoteuses, Fileuses, Poissardes—shouting, gesticulating, screaming the "Marseillaise" or the "Ça Ira" with their wild, demoniac voices, as they watched the red cart deposit its living freight at the foot of the National Razor. When hunger pressed them very sore, they would snatch up swords, pikes, or scythes, and rush in crowds along the narrow, muddy, ill-paved streets, beating drums, waving red flags, brandishing their weapons, to demand bread from those who professed to guide the Republic.

There was always some female leader, brave and eloquent, round whom the Furies would rally, and who was, if possible, more bloodthirsty, more ruthless than the rest. The great leaders of the Parisian Women were Rose Lacombe, the actress, and Théroigne (or Lambertine) de Méricourt, the Amazon of Liége. These two women, equally beautiful, equally brave, and equally popular, had wholly different reasons for plunging into the seething whirlpool of blood. Rose Lacombe (who was born in 1768, and was therefore past twenty when the Revolution broke out), appears to have joined in the scenes of atrocity through a love of excitement, a wish to be a leader, that feeling so natural in the breast of an actress. She was a wild, excitable girl, and although not great on the stage, had a certain fiery eloquence, which, though bombastic, exaggerated, even grotesque, was suited to an audience chiefly gathered from the Halles. Théroigne de Méricourt, however, had quite another object in coming forward as a Republican leader; this was an unquenchable thirst for revenge on the entire aristocracy, to one of whom she owed the shame of her life.

Théroigne was the daughter of a wealthy farmer in the village of Méricourt near Liége, and received a finished education. When scarcely seventeen her excessive beauty attracted the notice of a young Belgian noble, who owned a château close by her father's home. In those days of the old *régime* an aristocrat would never have recovered the disgrace of marrying a farmer's daughter; so the consequences of their mutual passion might easily have been foreseen. Deserted by her lover, Théroigne fled to England, and remained here for some months, in an agony of shame and grief. When Paris rose against the ill-starred Louis Seize, she returned to France, and became acquainted with Mirabeau, and through him she was introduced to to the Abbé Siéyes, Joseph Chénier, Brissac, Danton, Marat, Robespierre, Camille Desmoulins, Ronsin, Romme, and others of the Republican party.

Théroigne de Méricourt was barely eighteen in '89, when the first rumblings of the storm were heard. Plunging headlong into the vortex of Revolution, she soon acquired for her daring the names of "the Amazon of Liége" and "the Jeanne d'Arc of the Revolution;" while her surpassing beauty procured for her the title of "La Belle Liégoise." Attired in a blood-coloured silk riding-habit, and a hat surmounted by a magnificent plume of feathers, she made herself conspicuous in all those deadly conflicts between the People and the Royalists. She was first amongst the infuriate mob who burst open the gates of the Invalides and seized the cannon. She was foremost in the storming of the Bastille, June 14th, 1789; and such was her reckless valour on this occasion, that the victors, assembling on the spot, voted her a *sabre d'homme*. Another of the heroines who joined in the attack on the Bastille, afterwards joined the army, and fought against the enemies of the Republic, for which she was made Captain of Artillery. Her husband was a soldier.

On the 5th of October, Théroigne and Rose led eight or ten thousand starving Parisian Women against Versailles. Previous to this, Rose had commanded a body of Furies in the attack on the Hôtel de Ville, August 7th. Théroigne rode to Versailles astride on a cannon. By her side came Cut-Throat Jourdan, the " Man with the Long Beard." The expedition owed its success almost entirely to the Amazon of Liége. The triumph of the people was complete. *Le Boulanger, la Boulangère, et le petit Mitron* were brought to Paris, escorted by a seething, howling mob, preceded (as a hint to the aristocrats) by two pikes, on which were placed the heads of two Gardes-du-Corps. Several Poissardes performed the return journey on the backs of cannon.

For a time the popularity of Théroigne de Méricourt and Rose Lacombe was unbounded; they were estimated by the Parisians as the first of their sex. Rose founded a female club on the same plan as the Jacobins, and became the chief speaker there. Théroigne held a club at her own house, and frequently spoke at the "Old Cordeliers," of which Danton and Camille Desmoulins were the leaders. Speaking of the enthusiasm with which her orations were received, Camille says "Her similes were drawn from the Bible and Pindar. It was the eloquence of a Judith."

One evening Théroigne proposed that the Temple of the Representatives of the People should be erected on the site of the Bastille, the scene of their first triumph.

"To found and embellish this edifice," said she, "let us strip ourselves of our ornaments, our gold, our jewels. I will be the first to set the example."

And with these words she tore off all her jewels and flung them on the table.

Her power increased every day. She was appointed commander of the 3rd corps of the army of the Fauxbourgs; and so great was her ascendancy over the mob, that she could by a single word acquit or condemn a victim. She thus became both feared and hated by the Aristocrats. One day when she was at the zenith of her power, she recognised her faithless lover. He sought to avert his impending fate and humbly implored her forgiveness; but Théroigne had not the generosity to save him. He perished in the September massacres, 1792.

A fearful doom was reserved for the beautiful and unfortunate Théroigne de Méricourt. Like Robespierre, she believed that her power was such that she could at any moment arrest the progress of the Revolution. Only a few months after the death of her seducer, the very Furies whom she had commanded, by whom she had been almost worshipped, suspecting her of being a Girondist, turned against their Amazon leader with all the fury they had formerly displayed against Marie Antoinette. They surrounded her on the terrace of the Tuileries, May 31st, 1793, stripped her naked, and subjected her to a public flogging.

Abandoned and despised by all, the beautiful amazon became a raving lunatic. Years crept on. The Directory superseded the Convention, the Consulate the Directory, the Empire the Consulate, and the Restoration the Empire, and still, in a cold grated cell of the Bicêtre, in Paris, a gibbering, white-haired, wrinkled hag crawled on all fours to and from the bars of the window, whence she shrieked forth warlike orations to phantom meetings of Republicans; again and again calling for the blood of Suleau, the Royalist author. From the day of her fall till her death in 1817, she refused to wear clothes. Her only covering was her long white hair.

Rose Lacombe terminated her career more happily than her sister-in-arms. True, she also had her downfall, but it did not terminate so horribly. She fell violently in love with a young nobleman who was imprisoned in one of the dungeons of the Republic. With her usual wild impetuosity she tried to save him; but so far from rescuing him, she very nearly shared his fate. From this day Rose Lacombe's power was gone. Her voice was no longer listened to as it had once been. Jacobins and Cordeliers no longer strove to gain her support. Taking a more sensible view of the matter than one would expect, she retired from public life, and became a small shopkeeper. In this capacity she ended her days, selling petty articles over a counter all day long. The date of her death is unknown.

The citizens of Lyons, unlike those of Paris, were devoted to the Royal cause. At last the Convention resolved to tolerate this no longer; and General Kellermann was despatched against the city in August, 1793. The people made a gallant defence; never did the female sex show greater bravery. The city fell on Oct. 8th; and, furious at having been resisted, Collot d'Herbois, Couthon, and the other emissaries of the Convention tried to stamp out the very existence of Lyons. Wholesale massacres were perpetrated daily ; and the friends of liberty were if possible more enraged against those brave women, who so nobly aided in the defence, than they were against the male leaders. One of the most intrepid female soldiers, named Madame Cochet, when she was on her way to the guillotine, addressed her countrymen from the tumbril, and upbraided them with their cruelty, and their cowardice in tamely submitting to the Terrorists. The crowd at first followed in silence ; at last a cry of " Mercy," was heard : but the falling of the National Razor cut short the appeal.

Another heroine of Lyons was Marie Adrian, a young girl of seventeen, whose features bore a strange resemblance to Charlotte Corday. She fought desperately by the side of her brother and her lover in one of the batteries. After the city had fallen she was made prisoner.

" What is your name ? " demanded the judges, struck by her youth and beauty.

" Marie," she replied. " The name of the mother of that God for whom I am about to die."

" Your age ? "

" Seventeen. The age of Charlotte Corday."

" How could you combat against your country ? "

" I fought to defend it."

"Citoyenne," said one of the judges, "we admire your courage. What would you do if we granted your life?"

"I would poignard you as the murderers of my country," was her daring reply.

She was, of course, condemned to the guillotine. She ascended the scaffold in silence, and refused the aid of the executioner. Twice she cried with a loud, clear voice "Vive le Roi!" After her death a note was found among her garments; it was the farewell letter of her lover, who had been shot some days previously in the Plaine des Brotteaux.

This letter was written in blood!

The same loyal, unselfish courage was displayed by the Royalist insurgents in La Vendée. The rough, yet kind-hearted Chouans form a striking contrast to the ferocious, bloodthirsty Republicans, far from advantageous to the latter. There was not one Republican leader who could bear comparison with the enthusiastic self-sacrificing young Rochejacquelin, who risked everything for his King.

The most prominent Vendéan leaders, next to Rochejacquelin, were La Rochefoucault de Beaulieu and the Marquis de Lescure. The former was one of the first to raise the standard of Louis XVIII. Scarcely had he called together a few hundred neighbours and their peasant tenantry when he received a visit from Madlle. de la Rochefoucault, a near relative, and at this time only eighteen. She was accoutred *en Amazon*, with a sword by her side and a brace of pistols in her belt. She presented the troops with embroidered standards, worked by her own hands, and declared her resolution to fight personally for the royal cause.

Mademoiselle de la Rochefoucault displayed the greatest possible daring in the numerous encounters between the contending armies. She was always the first to advance and the last to retreat. But though she was so fierce while the battle raged, directly it was over she showed her kind and humane disposition by the care which she took of the wounded. She made no distinction between friends and foes; the unfortunate, whether Royalists or Republicans, were always sure of her sympathy and assistance.

In the disastrous battle of Chollet, when the superior numbers of the Republicans spread such confusion through the Chouan ranks, Mademoiselle de la Rochefoucault rallied her troops three times successively, and charged the foe. Repulsed a fourth time, she ascended a slight eminence, and addressed seven hundred of her followers in a speech well calculated to rouse their sinking energies. Once more she led them against the foe. This time they returned without her!

But the most famous heroine of this war was Renée Bordereau, commonly called Langevin, known as the "Military Heroine of La Vendée," who afterwards wrote and published her autobiography. She was born in June, 1770, at the village of Soulaine, near Angers, of poor, but honest parents. When the insurrection of 1793 broke out, the Republican troops ravaged and massacred without mercy throughout La Vendée. It chanced that forty-two of Renée's relatives fell victims, successively, to this fury. At last the barbarous murder of her father before her eyes so transported Renée with rage and a thirst for revenge that she devoted herself thenceforth to the royal cause.

She bought a light musket with double sights, and learned privately to load, fire, and aim at a mark. She also practised the military drill; and when she considered herself sufficiently expert, she procured a suit of masculine clothes, and joined a corps commanded by M. Cœur-de-Roi—whose name, by the way, was only a *nom de guerre*. She enrolled under the name of Hyacinthe, that of her brother, but her comrades soon gave her the soubriquet of Langevin, a name she never lost.

During a war of six years, the ·heroine was engaged in over two hundred battles and skirmishes. She usually fought on horseback, but sometimes, to be nearer the foe, she combated on foot. She always solicited to be placed in the most dangerous posts, and never quitted the field till compelled by her wounds, or the toils and fatigues of the battle. Although no one at this time suspected her sex, she was conspicuous all through the country for her bravery. All the Royalists strove to emulate her deeds of valour, but none could ever equal her daring. She had entered on the war with a firm determination to conquer or die, and her resolution never flagged. Her only ambition, her sole passion, was to drive the Republicans from France, and restore the legitimate Church and King.

When Napoleon had subdued La Vendée, he was so afraid of the brave Langevin that he excepted her from the general amnesty, and set the price of forty million francs on her head. She was betrayed into the hands of her enemies; and the Emperor threw her into a loathsome dungeon, weighting her limbs with iron chains lest she should escape. She remained in the prison of Angers for three years, and in that of Mount St. Michael for two, and was fed on nothing save the coarsest bread, and rainwater which she collected for herself in a basin. Her piety and fortitude, however, never forsook her during these cruel hardships. She was at last set free on the Restoration of that King for whom she had fought so bravely and endured such privations.

The sex of Renée had become known by an accident before her imprisonment; so it was no surprise, at least to her comrades, when her autobiography appeared, to learn that she was a woman. In 1816, she was presented to Louis XVIII.; but what recompense if any, was awarded, her memoirs do not say. She was still living in 1818.

Madame Dufief, a native of Nantes, was another heroine of this war; and, in reward she received at the Restoration the Ribbon of the Order of St. Louis.

The French Revolution, it must be confessed, aroused throughout the land a feeling of earnest, self-sacrificing patriotism, which no monarchical government, however popular, had ever called forth. A wild, enthusiastic desire spread through France to drive the enemies of the Republic from its sacred soil or perish in the attempt. Young and old were alike infected with the eager longing to die for the Republic. "Married men," says Lamartine, "dragged themselves from the arms of their wives to rush to the altar of their country. Men already advanced in life, old men, even, still green and robust, came to offer the remainder of their life to the safety of the Republic. They were seen tearing off their coats or jackets, before the representatives, and exposing, naked, their breasts, their shoulders, their arms, their joints still supple, to prove that they had strength enough to carry the knapsack and the carbine, and to brave the fatigues of the camp. Fathers, devoting themselves with their children, themselves offered their sons to the country, and demanded to be allowed to march with them. Women, in order to follow their husbands or their lovers, or themselves seized with that delirium of the country, the most generous and the most devoted of all passions, divested themselves of the garments of their sex, put on the uniform of volunteers, and enrolled themselves in the battalions of their departments."

The greater number of these brave women and girls left their bones to bleach on the various battle-fields of the Republic without their sex being ever discovered. Those who became known were but few. Amongst these latter were the two sisters Félicité and Théophile de Fernig, who held the nominal rank of orderly officers on the staff of General Dumouriez, wearing the uniform, and performing all the duties appertaining to their position. Their father, M. de Fernig, was Captain of Dumouriez's Guides; while their brother was lieutenant in the regiment d'Auxerrois. Thus the entire family were fighting in defence of the Republic.

The De Fernigs were natives of French Flanders, whence they were driven in August, 1792, by the invading Austrians, who amongst other atrocities, burnt the house of this family. Having no longer a home, they joined the army of Dumouriez which arrived shortly after in the neighbourhood. The girls, whose sex was known to all, when on the march rode near their father or brother; but during battle they acted as aide-de-camp to one or other of the French generals.

They entered at once on active service, and marched to the woody heights of Argonne in Champagne, which General Dumouriez was vainly endeavouring to hold against the Austrians. On his retreat to St. Ménéhould the De Fernigs distinguished themselves, September 20th, during the famous cannonade of Valmy by the Duke of Brunswick; when the superior skill of Kellermann forced the Allies to retreat.

The Convention, informed of the gallant conduct of the Desmoiselles de Fernig, sent them horses and arms of honour in the name of the Republic. Dumouriez, in the camp of Maulde, made a striking example of these two young girls to inspire his soldiers with courage.

In October, Dumouriez returned to Paris, and formed a plan with the Executive Council for the winter campaign. On his return to the army he issued a proclamation calling on the Belgians to rise against their sovereign; and on the 6th of November, he attacked the Austrian camp at Jemappes. In this battle, which was perhaps the most hotly contested of all those fought during the entire war, Félicité, the eldest girl, acted as aide-de-camp to the Duc de Chartres, afterwards Louis Philippe, King of the French, while her sister performed the same duty for the brave veteran, General Ferrand, who stormed the redoubts on the heights. Both girls were young and exceedingly pretty—Félicité was scarcely sixteen; and "their modesty, their blushes, and their grace," observed Lamartine, "under the uniform of officers of the staff, formed a contrast to the masculine figures of the warriors who surrounded them."

Before the battle, while reviewing his troops, Dumouriez pointed out the heroines to his soldiers "as models of patriotism and auguries of victory." Throughout the day they were conspicuous for their reckless bravery, which rendered them of inestimable price in an army composed of raw soldiers. When the regiments which formed the centre of the French army gave way before the overwhelming masses of Clerfayt's cavalry, the Duc de Chartres and his brother, the Duc de Montpensier, followed by Félicité de Fernig and half-a-dozen aides-de-camp, rode, sword in hand, through the Austrian hussars' which separated him from the infantry. The latter were restored to their former courage, partly by the words of the Duc, but more especially by the reproaches of a fragile girl of sixteen, who, a pistol in each hand and her bridle between her teeth, accused them bitterly of cowardice in flying from dangers which she fearlessly braved.

After the battle had raged for several hours the Austrians were driven from the field. The capture of Mons followed shortly after; and the French entered Brussels, November 14th, after a series of skirmishes between their advance-guard and the rear-guard of the Austrians. During one of these contests, Félicité de Fernig, while bearing the orders of Dumouriez to the heads of the columns, was surrounded by a troop of Uhlans, from whom she extricated herself with difficulty. As she was turning her horse's head to rejoin the column, she saw a young officer of Belgian Volunteers, who had just been flung from his horse, by a shot, defending himself desperately against several Uhlans. Riding hastily to the spot, Félicité with her pistols shot two of his assailants, and the rest took to flight.

Dismounting from her horse, she confided the care of the wounded officer to her hussars, and with their assistance conveyed him to the military hospital of Brussels.

The spring of 1793 saw the popularity of Dumouriez wane rapidly. He was suspected firstly of Girondism, and, worse again, of wishing to rescue

Louis Capet, the unfortunate ex-King, whose trial was in preparation, or, some said, he meditated placing Philippe Egalité on the throne. In addition to all these accusations, he had the misfortune to lose nearly as many battles as he had previously gained; and, knowing well that his head was very far from secure on his martial shoulders, he entered into negotiations with Austria. But he mistook the patriotism of his soldiers for personal attachment to himself. On the 7th April his army was in a state of open mutiny; but hoping to set matters right, he set out for Condé, followed by the Duc de Chartres, Colonel Thouvenet, Adjutant-General Montjoie, eight hussars of ordnance, and his immediate staff, including the sisters De Fernig. On the road he met three battalions of Versailles Volunteers who were marching without orders to Condé. Dumouriez commanded them to halt; but the Volunteers fired on his escort. Dumouriez fled amidst a rain of bullets, sprang, on foot, across a canal which interrupted his flight, and made his escape over the Dutch marshes.

Théophile de Fernig was not wounded, though her horse was slain. Félicité dismounted, and gave her steed to the Duc de Chartres. The two young girls and nearly all their companions reached the opposite shore of the canal safely; when they dispersed in all directions. The girls, who were acquainted with the country, guided Dumouriez to the ferry-boat, in which he, they, and the Duc de Chartres passed the Scheldt. On landing they returned to the French camp at Maulde; but very soon the fugitives had to take refuge in the camp of Clerfayt, the Austrian general, at Tournay.

In those days one star eclipsed another so fast, that the soldiers were only too ready to forget their former idols. Of course when the troops could easily forget the general who had first led them to victory, they could hardly be expected to trouble themselves about two friendless girls. When Vanderwalen, the young Belgian officer, recovered from his wounds, he could not banish from his mind the young Amazon who had saved his life. But neither his brother officers nor the soldiers could give him any information respecting the De Fernig family. Vanderwalen left the army, and wandered all over Germany and northern Europe seeking his preserver. For a long time his search was vain; but at last, when he had almost given up the search, he found the family buried in the heart of Denmark.

The sisters had resumed "the dress, the graces, and the modesty" of their own sex. The love of Vanderwalen was very soon reciprocated; and they returned, as man and wife, to Belgium. Théophile accompanied her sister to Brussels; where, after spending a few years in the study of music and poetry, she died, unmarried. She has left, it is said, several exquisite poems.

"These two sisters," says Lamartine, "inseparable in life, in death, as upon the field of battle, repose under the same cypress—in a foreign land. Where are their names upon the marble monuments of our triumphal arches? Where are their pictures at Versailles? Where are their statues upon our frontiers bedewed with their blood?"

Mary Schelienck, or Shellenck, was one of the most remarkable women whose names occur in the roll-call of warriors. She was a native of Ghent, but nothing is known of her early youth. In March, 1792, she entered the Second Belgian Battalion, as a male Volunteer. At the battle of Jemappes, in the succeeding November, she distinguished herself by her bravery, and received six wounds. Afterwards she entered the 30th Demi-Brigade (Batavian), and made the campaigns of Germany. She was next removed to the 8th Light Infantry, and displayed great bravery at the battle of Austerlitz. Unfortunately for her, she there received a severe wound on the thigh, and was left for dead on the field, which led to her real sex being discovered. In spite of this, she continued to follow the regiment, and at last presented a petition with her own hand to Napoleon. The Emperor received her with "marked distinction:" he invested her with the cross of the Legion of Honour, giving her the very decoration he had himself worn, and he placed her tenth on the list of lieutenants. In 1807, Napoleon granted her a pension of 673 francs (£20). On her return from Italy, Mary Schelienck, in her military uniform, waited on the Empress Josephine. That imperial lady, either in kindness or as an ironical compliment, presented her with a velvet robe. Mary Schelienck's commission of lieutenant, the decoration of the Legion of Honour, and the velvet robe were afterwards (1841) in the possession of William Shellenck, cloth merchant of Ghent. Mary Shelienck died in January, 1841, at Menin, where she was buried. Her funeral was attended by every member of the Legion of Honour belonging to the garrison, and an immense concourse of people.

Thérèse Figueur, better known as "Le Dragon sans Gêne," was born, January, 1774, at Talmay, a town six leagues from Dijon. She became a dragoon in the 15th and 9th regiments, and, from 1793 to 1812, served in all the campaigns of the Republic and of the Empire. At this time she was known to her comrades by the soubriquet of "Sans Gêne."

One day the Comité du Salut Public issued a decree forbidding any woman to remain in the regiments. The commissioned officers and generals of the army of the Pyrenees, however, begged that an exception might be made in favour of the Citoyenne Thérèse Figueur; and special authorization was granted, permitting her to remain in the service.

At the siege of Toulon, 1793, Thérèse received an English bullet in her left shoulder. She had the misfortune to be placed under arrest during the same siege by General Bonaparte, for being guilty of a delay of twenty-five minutes in the execution of an order. Some years subsequently, when the former Commandant d'Artillerie had become First Consul, he wished to see once more the Dragon sans Gêne, who came willingly enough to St. Cloud under the escort of M. Denon. The First Consul made some complimentary remarks to the " Dragon," and added that " Mademoiselle Figueur est un brave : " then gaily pledged her in " a glass of something stronger than wine."

Thérèse Figueur served in the " Armée d'Italie " in 1792, and in the army of the Eastern Pyrenees during the 2nd and 3rd year, and in the Army of Italy during the years 4, 5, 6, 7, 8, and 9. Among her exploits were several campaigns in Germany, and she took part in the war in Spain. In July, 1812, she was made prisoner by the Guerillas of the Curé Marino, and sent off to England, where she remained until the Peace in 1814.

She was frequently wounded, and had horses

killed under her. At the battle of Savigliano, she was wounded four times.

A modest pension hardly sufficed for her simple wants, yet being very generous, she constantly helped others poorer than herself. In disposition she was remarkable for piety, delicate tact, singleness of heart, and self-forgetfulness.

About 1840, Thérèse Figueur, then *veuve* Sutter, was admitted into the Hospice des Ménages. In that retreat her last years glided calmly away, enlivened by the frequent visits of her many faithful friends, who delighted in hearing her military reminiscences. In June, 1861, her simple funeral passed from the gates of the Hospice.

During the long wars between England and the French Republic, women continued to enlist in the British Army. One of the best known female soldiers of this period was a woman named Roberts, afterwards styled the " Manchester Heroine " from the place of her death. On the 15th November, 1814, a middle-aged woman applied for relief at the Church-Warden's offices in Manchester; and on being questioned, it appeared that she had in days gone by served her King as a soldier. Her romantic story afterwards appeared, in great detail, in the *Manchester Herald*.

The father of this heroine, William Roberts, was

a bricklayer, and used to employ his little girl, dressed in boy's clothes, as a labourer. When she was about fourteen years old, being tall of her age, Miss Roberts enlisted in the 15th Light Dragoons. In the course of two months she learned the drill sufficiently for all purposes of parade; and the rough-riding master told her she was the best rider in the squad he was teaching. Private William Roberts was promoted in the course of a few years, first to be a corporal, and then a sergeant; and at the expiration of her twenty-one years' service, the colonel tendered her discharge. She demurred accepting it; but being under size, was, with her own consent, transferred to the 37th foot; which she joined at the island of St. Vincent, in the West Indies.

At St. Vincent the heroine was attacked by the yellow fever; and this being the first time in her life that she was ever laid prostrate by an illness, her sex was soon made known. On her recovery she was obliged to resume (or rather put on) female habilaments. But being still enamoured of a soldier's life, she married, in May, 1801, a private in the 37th, named Taylor. She followed her husband through various climates; and in time became the mother of three children. She was imprisoned for two years with her husband in France, and they were only set free at the general peace of July, 1815. Her husband died the same day they landed in England; leaving his widow in great distress.

During the course of her military career, Mrs. Taylor visited the East and West Indies, and fought in Flanders, Spain, Italy, and Egypt. She received many wounds, none of which, however, were serious, though they left their scars all over her body. Her head was graced by a sabre-wound, while her leg showed where a musket ball had ben extracted. Yet despite the dangers and hardships of war, this woman sighed after the life of a soldier to the very last. She said that the only really miserable part of her life was the two years' imprisonment in France; which, she said, did her constitution more harm than even the terrible march, under a blazing African sun, from the Red Sea to Egypt. Like a brave old veteran, she kept up her spirits even in adversity, "fought her battles o'er again," and loved to "shoulder her crutch and show how fields were won." Like most old soldiers, she was very fond of relating anecdotes about her past career—the battles she had fought in, the wounds she had received, and the various noble or distinguished officers she had seen.

Another of these British heroines was Mary Anne Talbot, who served as drummer-boy in the 82nd regiment when it was despatched to the Netherlands in 1793. The career of this young woman was so romantic, so very much out of the ordinary routine of every-day life, it is strange that her story has not become more generally known—especially as a long and detailed memoir was published, which she was supposed to have written herself.

Mary Anne Talbot was born in a house in Lincoln's Inn Fields on the 2nd February, 1778, and was the youngest of sixteen natural children, whom her mother, whose name has not transpired, had by the Earl of Talbot. Until she had reached the age of five, Mary Anne was kept at nurse at a little village about twelve miles from Shrewsbury. Her mother died when she was an infant; and at the death of Lord Talbot, Mary Anne was removed to a boarding-school in Foregate-street, Chester. Here she remained for nine years under the care of her only surviving sister, Mrs. Wilson. On the death of Mrs. Wilson, Mr. Sucker, of Newport, Shropshire, came forward as guardian of Mary Anne Talbot. He was a harsh man, and treated her so cruelly that she trembled at the sound of his voice. She had not been in her new home very long when Essex Bowen, a captain in the 82nd, appeared at the house; and the girl was commanded by Sucker to consider him as her future guardian, under whose protection she was to finish her education on the continent.

Early in the year 1792 they proceeded to London and stopped at the Salopian coffee-house, Charing Cross; where, taking advantage of the poor girl's friendless situation, Captain Bowen acted the part of a villain. Immediately after this the 82nd was ordered to the West Indies; and the captain forced his victim to dress herself as a foot-boy and follow him. By his directions, too, she assumed the name of John Taylor. They sailed on the 20th March, from Falmouth, in the Crown Transport ; and during the voyage her tyrant used her like a slave, and forced her to eat and drink with the common sailors.

Early in the following year the regiment was remanded to Europe, to join the army of the Duke of York at Tournay. Bowen again intimidating the forlorn girl by the threat of sending her up the country to be sold for a slave, compelled her to enlist under him as a drummer, though he plainly told her that this would not release her from her duties as his servant.

When they arrived in Flanders, Mary Anne was obliged to endure all the horrors of war. During the frequent skirmishes which took place between the English and French, she was compelled to keep up a continuous roll of the drum to drown the groans and cries of wounded and dying comrades. On the 2nd of June, the Duke of York besieged Valenciennes;

within a few days of its surrender, the female drummer received two wounds—one from a musket-ball which glanced between her collar-bone and breast-bone, and struck one of her ribs, the other in the small of her back from the sabre of an Austrian trooper, who mistook her for a Frenchman. Being in dread and fear lest her sex should be discovered, she had the fortitude to conceal her wounds, and cure them herself by the use of some lint, Dutch drops and basilicon.

Captain Bowen had the reward of his villany and tyranny, by being slain during the attack on Valenciennes, July 25th, 1793. Having no longer the wrath of a tyrant to fear, Mary Anne disguised herself as a sailor boy, deserted from the regiment, and started for the coast. Carefully avoiding all towns or large villages, she reached Luxembourg, which being in the hands of the French, hindered her further progress. She was compelled, through sheer want, to hire herself to the captain of a French lugger. The vessel turned out to be a privateer, and cruised about the Channel for four months. Mary Anne was compelled to do all the rough work. At last the vessel was captured by the British fleet, and the crew were taken prisoners on board the " Queen Charlotte " to be examined by the admiral, Lord Howe. Previous to their capture, Mary Anne was severely beaten because she refused to fight against her countrymen.

Lord Howe questioned Mary Anne as to who and what she was, and how she had got on board a French ship. She stated, in explanation, that she had been foot-boy to an English gentleman travelling on the continent, that on his death she had been obliged to seek employment, and had taken Le Sage the French captain, for an honest trader. The Admiral was satisfied; and the girl was sent on board the "Brunswick" man-of-war, where she was appointed powder-monkey on the quarter-deck. Her cleanly habits, and her quiet respectful demeanour, attracted the notice of Captain Harvey, who raised her to the post of principal cabin boy.

The "Brunswick" having fallen in with a French ship, in June, 1794, a sharp action ensued, in which Captain Harvey was slain, and Mary Anne received a grape-shot in the ankle of her left leg. So severe was the wound that, though she tried three several times to rise, the broken bone protruding through the skin gave her such agony she fell back almost fainting. A few minutes after this a musket-ball pierced her thigh, just above the knee of the same leg. After the engagement she was carried to the cock-pit, and after numberless attempts had been made to extract the grape-shot (inflicting excruciating agony all the while on the sufferer), the surgeons were obliged to leave it where it was, fearful of cutting the tendons of the leg.

When the "Brunswick" arrived at Spithead, Mary Anne Talbot was placed in Haslar Hospital, where she was attended as an out-door patient during four months. She lived meanwhile on the money which Captain Harvey had given her. When she was at last discharged from the Hospital, she went as a midshipman on board the "Vesuvius," which formed part of Sir Sydney Smith's squadron. After cruising some time on the coast of France the "Vesuvius" sailed to Gibraltar and back again without meeting the enemy until near Dunkirk, where she was boarded and captured by two privateers, after keeping up a running fight for seven hours.

Mary Anne and another middy named William Richards were taken on board one of the privateers, and imprisoned for eighteen months in Dunkirk, where they were treated very harshly—being allowed nothing but bread and water, and a bed of straw which was never changed. An exchange of prisoners took place at last; and Mary Anne Talbot was engaged almost immediately after by a Captain Field to go as ship's steward on a voyage to America.

She sailed from Dunkirk on board the "Ariel," August, 1796, and arrived in due time at New York. During her stay there she resided in the family of Captain Field at Rhode Island; and the pretty niece of the captain was so absurd as to fall in love with her uncle's steward. Before Mary Anne's departure she was obliged to pay eighteen dollars for a portrait of herself in the uniform of an American officer to give to her affianced as a memento.

The "Ariel" dropped anchor in the Thames in November, 1796; and some days after their arrival, Mary Anne and the mate went on shore, where they were seized by the press-gang. To obtain her freedom she was obliged to reveal her sex.

Mary Anne applied several times at the Navy-Pay Office for moneys due to her for service on board the "Brunswick" and "Vesuvius." One day she became abusive, and was taken to Bow Street Police Court; whence of course she was very soon discharged. Several gentlemen who were in court made up a subscription, the amount of which was twelve shillings a week, to last until she received her pension from Somerset House.

Mary Anne Talbot wasted her money shamefully at the theatres and at certain public-houses near Covent Garden, where her real sex was not even suspected; all her friends giving her the name of *bon compagnon*. In February, 1797, owing to her fondness for grog, the grape-shot worked itself out of her ankle, and left her leg in so bad a state that she was taken into St. Bartholomew's Hospital. After her discharge she was attended in different hospitals by several medical men, none of whom were able to effect a permanent cure. She became at last so famous that a beggar was sent to the House of Correction charged with passing himself off as John Taylor, the midshipman. In 1799, she became, for the second time, an inmate of Middlesex Hospital.

For some years her principal support was a pension of twenty pounds a year from the Crown; besides this she received frequent presents from the Duke of York, the Duke of Norfolk, and other members of the nobility. She was advised by Justice Bond, the magistrate of Bow Street, to endeavour to find out something about her early life. She went to Shrewsbury and called on Mr. Sucker, in Newport. Being unable to procure an interview while in " coloured " clothes, she returned to Shrewsbury, dressed herself in an ensign's uniform, hired a horse, and rode back to Mr. Sucker's. She sent in word that an officer, a friend of the late Captain Bowen, had an important message to deliver. This *ruse* succeeded; she declared who she was, and, drawing her sword, demanded an explanation of Mr. Sucker's conduct towards her. He stared as though an apparition had risen from the grave, and, trembling violently, repeated that he was a ruined man. Three days after this he was found dead in his bed.

Mary Anne Talbot lived for many years after this, maintaining herself in various ways. At one time she thought of going on the stage, and joined the Thespian Society in Tottenham Court Road; where she performed the parts of Irene, Lady Helen, Juliet, Floranthe, and Adeline, and sometimes appeared in low comedy as Mrs. Scout, or Jack Hawser. However, she gave up the stage, which was to her more amusing than profitable.

Once she was summoned before the Commissioners of the Stamp Office for wearing hair-powder without a licence. But she was honourably discharged; whereupon she made the observation that "although she had never worn powder as an article of dress, she had frequently used it in defence of her King and country." The clerks were so tickled with her wit that they immediately made up a subscription.

In June, 1796, the British attacked the New Vigie, in the Island of St. Vincent. The Royal Highlanders were conspicuous for their valour, as Highlanders have ever been. Major-General Stewart, at that time a captain in the regiment, relates how one of the men of his company was followed to the scene of action by his wife. He (Captain Stewart) ordered the man to remain behind and guard the knapsacks, which the soldiers threw down preparatory to charging up the hill. The woman, however, perhaps thinking that the family honour was at stake, rushed up the hill, and made herself conspicuous, cheering and exciting the troops. When the British had captured the third redoubt, Captain Stewart was standing at a short distance, giving some directions relative to the storming of the last entrenchments, when he was tapped on the shoulder by the female Highlander, who seized his arm, and exclaimed:

"Well done, my Highland lads! See how the brigands scamper like so many deer! Come, lads, let us drive them from yonder hill."

And she charged off again, much to the delight of her Gaelic brothers-in-arms. When the storm was over, she helped the surgeons in looking after the wounded.

During the Irish Rebellion of '98, women very often risked their lives both on the battle-field and in the defence of houses. Amongst the latter was Susan Frost, a Suffolk woman, nurse to General Sir Charles James Napier. During the temporary absence of the Napier family in England, this woman remained at Celbridge House, in Ireland, with a few of the younger children. The "Defenders" having ascertained that this mansion contained a great number of arms, surrounded it one night. The only persons in the house, besides Susan and the children, were a few maids and Lauchlin Moore, an old serving-man. The rebels, who numbered several hundreds, anticipated an easy capture; but the house was strongly built, and, besides, was defended by Susan Frost, of whose obstinate courage they were as yet ignorant. Collecting all the children together in one room, she stationed herself with a brace of pistols outside the door. The "Defenders" called on the little garrison to surrender; but Lauchlin Moore, acting under the orders of Susan, shouted out defiant refusals. Every time he passed a window, volleys of shot whizzed around his head.

When the assailants began to batter the door with a beam of wood, Moore's courage failed him, and he wished to give up the arms. But Susan invariably answered "No! No! Never! Never!" At last the arrival of some men-servants, from a neighbouring mansion, put the rebels to flight.

Another heroine of the Irish Rebellion was Peggy Monro, who fought bravely in the battle of Ballinahinch, where the rebels were commanded by her brother.

At the latter end of 1797 the French invaded Switzerland, with the ostensible view of spreading liberty, equality, and fraternity. However, in place of being welcomed by the republican Swiss, they were met on all sides by armed peasants who defended every foot of ground before giving way. The women acted with the same courage as the men. The most conspicuous was Martha Glar, a peasant-woman. When the war broke out she was far from young; being then in her sixty-fourth year, and having both children and grandchildren.

In February, 1798, her husband marched with the rest of the farmers and peasants to check the advance of the French. On the last Sunday in the month, Martha collected all the women and girls of the parish in the church-yard, half an hour before divine service, and addressed them in an impressive oration, inciting them to take up arms in defence of their native land.

Two hundred and sixty women, urged by her patriotism, armed themselves, and marched to meet the invaders. In this little regiment were two of Martha Glar's daughters, and three of her granddaughters, the youngest of whom was only ten years old. After exciting the admiration of both friends and foes by their extraordinary bravery, this female corps was decimated in the battle of Frauenbrun, March 3rd, 1798. One hundred and eighty of them were killed, and the rest carried, more or less wounded, from the field. Martha Glar, together with her husband, her father, her two sons, both her daughters, her brother, and her three grand-daughters were amongst the slain.

In 1806, when Prussia was arming against the "Colossus of Europe," the Queen, who was young, beautiful, and fascinating, appeared several times at the head of the troops attired in a military uniform, which, it is said, became her exceedingly well; and in this costume she made fiery speeches inciting the people to rise against the "Modern Attila."

Besides this display of martial ardour, the Queen, mounted on a superb charger, accompanied the Prussian army to the field of Jena, Oct. 14th, 1806, and remained in the midst of the fight till her troops were routed. On her head she wore a helmet of burnished steel, overshadowed by a magnificent plume. She wore a tunic of silver brocade, reaching to her feet, which were encased in scarlet boots with gold spurs. Her breast was protected by a cuirass glittering in gold and silver. Accompanied by the *élite* of the young Berlin nobility, she rode along in front of the most advanced ranks, whence, the day being clear, she was easily seen by the French. As she approached each regiment, the flags, embroidered by her own fair hands, besides the blackened rags—all that remained of the time-honoured banners of Frederick the Great—were lowered respectfully.

When the battle was over and the Prussians in full rout, the Queen remained on the field, attended by three or four equerries, who, for some time, contrived to defend her against the French troops, who had strict orders to capture the Queen at all risks. A squadron of hussars riding up at full speed soon dispersed the little escort of her Majesty. The horse ridden by the Queen fortunately took fright, and galloped off at full speed. Had it not been for his swiftness, the royal heroine would inevitably have been captured.

Pursued by the detachment of hussars, who were several times within a few yards of the royal fugitive, she arrived at last within sight of Weimar, and was congratulating herself upon having escaped so imminent a danger, when, to her dismay, she observed a strong body of French dragoons endeavouring to cut off her retreat. However, before they could come near, she was inside Weimar, the gates of which were immediately closed upon the discomfited troopers.

The Queen found her costume exceedingly inconvenient during her flight; and it was principally owing to this that she was so very near being made prisoner.

Marie-Anne-Elise Bonaparte, sister of the first Napoleon, was a woman of superior intellect, and shared to a considerable extent her brother's military predilections. When she married Bacciochi, Prince of Lucca and Piombino, it was she who conducted the government, while the Prince was kept in a subordinate position. From her fondness for military shows she acquired the title of the "Semiramis of Lucca." Whenever she reviewed the troops, Prince Bacciochi discharged the duties of aide-de-camp.

Next to Joan of Arc, the Maid of Saragossa is the most famous female warrior that ever lived. Pictures and statues without number have been exhibited commemorative of this Spanish girl's heroism; and what renders her resemblance even greater to Jeanne is the fact that the Maid of Saragossa was young, handsome, and interesting.

The siege of Saragossa (or Zaragoza), was one of the most extraordinary recorded in modern history. The town was not even properly fortified, but merely enclosed by a badly-constructed wall twelve feet high and three feet in breadth. This was, moreover, intersected by houses, which, with the neighbouring churches and monasteries, were in a most dilapidated condition. The inhabitants numbered only sixty thousand, and amongst these there was barely two hundred and twenty soldiers. The artillery consisted of ten dilapidated old guns.

When the rest of Spain was at the feet of Napoleon, Marshal Lefebvre was despatched in June 1808, with a strong division of the French army to besiege Saragossa. Never, in our days at least, have the inhabitants of a beleaguered town displayed such courage. Women of all ranks assisted in the defence; they formed themselves into companies of two or three hundred each, and materially aided the men. They were always the most forward in danger, and the great difficulty was to teach them prudence and a proper sense of their own danger.

The French Marshal, astounded at this unexpected resistance, bribed the keeper of a large powder-magazine to blow it up on the night of June 28th. The French immediately pressed forward to the gates, and commenced a vigorous cannonade. The confusion within the walls was fearful. The people, terrified by the explosion, stupefied by the noise of the cannon thundering in their ears, were paralysed with terror. It was at this critical moment, when the French were pouring into the town, already considered it as their own, that Agostina (or Angostina) the Maid of Saragossa performed that heroic action which has made her name famous throughout the world.

According to the popular version of the story current at the time, the deed was unpremeditated, and simply the result of a sudden impulse. She was carrying round wine and water to the parched and fainting soldiers; entering the Battery of El Portillo, she found that all its defenders had been slain. She tore a match from the hand of a dying artilleryman (whom Southey incorrectly supposes to have been her lover) and fired off a twenty-six pounder gun which was loaded. But in Mrs. Hale's "Woman's Record," and some other biographical dictionaries, Agostina is represented as having gone to the battery with the previous determination of performing great deeds.

"At this dreadful moment," says Mrs. Hale, "an unknown maiden issued from the church of Nostra Donna del Pillas, habited in white raiment, a cross suspended from her neck, her dark hair dishevelled and her eyes sparkling with supernatural lustre! She traversed the city with a bold and firm step; she passed to the ramparts, to the very spot where the enemy was pouring in to the assault; she mounted to the breach, seized a lighted match from the hand of a dying engineer, and fired the piece of artillery he had failed to manage; then kissing her cross, she cried with the accent of inspiration— 'Death or victory!' and re-loaded her cannon. Such a cry, such a vision, could not fail to call up enthusiasm; it seemed that heaven had brought aid to the just cause; her cry was answered— 'Long live Agostina.'"

The people, inspired with new courage, rushed into the battery, and blazed away at the French. Agostina swore not to quit her post while the assault continued. The enthusiasm soon spread through the town. Shouts of "Forward! Forward! We will conquer!" resounded from all sides, and the besiegers were driven back at every point.

Marshal Lefebvre saw it would cost too many soldiers to take the town by storm; so he endeavoured to reduce it by famine, aided by a heavy bombardment. The horrors of war—people dying of hunger, shells bursting in the streets, the destruction of houses—reigned paramount in Saragossa. Agostina risked her life daily to assist the wounded. But she was seen daily working a heavy gun in the battery at the north-western gate.

The French, from their superior numbers and their determined perseverance, soon became masters of nearly half the town. Lefebvre sent to General Palafox, the Spanish Commandant, requesting him, once more, to surrender. Palafox read this message in the public street. Turning to Agostina, who, completely armed, stood near him, he asked:—
"What answer shall I send?"

"War to the knife!" said she.

And this answer, echoed by all, was sent back to the Duke of Dantzic.

The latter gave immediate orders for his troops to press the siege by every possible means. For eleven days and eleven nights the town was like the crater of a volcano. The Spaniards disputed the possession of every street, every house, sometimes every room in a house. Agostina was seen at all points, wherever there was most danger to be encountered. Running from post to post, she fought almost incessantly. At last the French, thoroughly exhausted, retired from before Saragossa early on the morning of the 17th August, and the brave townspeople had their reward when they saw the legions of France retiring towards Pampeluna.

When General Palafox was rewarding the surviving warriors, he told Agostina to select whatever reward she pleased; for, said he, anything she asked for would be granted. The only favour she asked was permission to retain the rank of an artillery-soldier, and to have the privilege of taking the surname, and wearing the arms of Saragossa. This was at once granted, with the double-pay of an artilleryman and a pension; while she was decorated with medals and crosses by the Spanish Junta, and given the additional surname of La Artillera.

During the second siege of Saragossa, Agostina distinguished herself again as a warrior. When the French sat down before the gates, she took up her former station at the Portillo battery, beside the same gun which she had served so well.

"See," said she to Palafox, pointing to the gun, "I am again with my old friend."

Her husband was severely wounded, but Agostina took his duties, while he lay bleeding at her side.

Besides loading and firing this famous gun, Agostina frequently headed sallying parties; when, knife or sword in hand, her cloak wrapped round her, she cheered and encouraged the soldiers by her example and her words. Although constantly under fire, she escaped without a wound. Once, however, she was flung into a ditch, and nearly suffocated by the bodies of dead and dying which fell upon her.

When the town capitulated in February, 1809, Agostina became a prisoner. She was too much feared for Marshal Lannes to let her escape. Fortunately for herself, she was seized with a contagious fever then raging in the town, and was removed to the hospital; where, as it was supposed she lay dying, so little care was taken in watching her that she contrived to escape in a few days.

When Lord Byron visited Spain in 1809, the maid of Saragossa used to walk every day on the Prado at Seville, attired in the Spanish military uniform— retaining, however, the petticoat and skirt, of her sex. Byron devoted half-a-dozen verses of "Childe Harold" to her praises. Sir John Carr, who was introduced to her about the same time, describes the heroine as "about twenty-three," with a light olive complexion. "Her countenance soft and pleasing, and her manners, which were perfectly feminine, were easy and engaging." When he saw Agostina she wore the national black mantilla; but on the sleeve of one arm she had three embroidered badges of honour, commemorative of three different acts of bravery.

"The day before I was introduced to this extraordinary female," says Sir John, "she had been entertained at dinner by Admiral Purvis on board his flag-ship.... As she received a pension from Government, and also the pay of an artilleryman, the admiral considered her as a military character, and, much to his credit, received her with the honours of that profession. Upon her reaching the deck, the marines were drawn up and manœuvred before her. She appeared quite at home, regarding them with a steady eye, and speaking in terms of admiration of their neatness, and soldier-like appearance. Upon examining the guns, she observed of one of them, as other women would speak of a cap, 'My gun,' alluding to one with which she had effected a considerable havoc among the French at Saragossa, 'was not so nice and clean as this.'"

Agostina lived to the age of sixty-nine, and died at Cuesta in July, 1857; when her remains were interred with all the honours due to her public position as a Spanish patriot.

Although the women of Saragossa had been ordered to leave the town in November, 1808, previous to the commencement of the second siege, most of them remained, and assisted bravely in raising fortifications. During the siege they exceeded even their past valour. In the short space of two months no fewer than six hundred women and children perished by the bayonets and musket-balls of the French; without reckoning the thousands who owed their deaths to the frequent explosions of powder-magazines and the constant bursting of shells in the streets. A girl named Manuella Sanchez was shot through the heart. A noble lady named Benita, who commanded one of the female corps raised to carry round provisions, to bear away the wounded, and to fight in the streets, narrowly escaped death again and again; and at the last she only survived the dangers of war to die of grief on hearing that her daughter had been slain.

All through the Peninsula women displayed the same Amazonian prowess. Those towns which ventured to resist the Imperial Eagles were as much influenced in their stubborn patriotism by the courage of the women as by the exciting speeches of the priests or the promise of assistance from England. And all those places which were besieged by the French were defended by women as well as by men. In 1810 there was, it is said, a woman holding the commission of Captain in a Spanish regiment.

In 1811, Mrs. Dalbiac, wife of a British colonel, "an English lady of gentle disposition and possessing a very delicate frame," accompanied, or perhaps followed, her husband to the Peninsula, and shared in all the hardships of more than one campaign. At the battle of Salamanca, July 22nd, 1812, she rode into the midst of the fight, and was several times under fire.

The King of Prussia, unable to shake off the yoke of Napoleon in 1806, when the star of the "Modern Attila" was at its zenith, took advantage of the Emperor's misfortunes in 1813 to call upon the Germans to rise against the tyranny of France. His call was warmly responded to from all parts of the realm; and, like France in the early days of the Republic, almost all who could bear arms hastened to enrol themselves as volunteers, and march away to fight the Gaul. Perhaps the best known rifle-corps was that commanded by Major Lutzow. Young men of the best families, men of genius (amongst others, Körner the poet, who has celebrated it in verse) joined this battalion. In this corps there was a female soldier, who enrolled under the name of Renz. A monument was erected to the memory of this heroine at Dannenberg, in September, 1865. It is in the form of a pyramid, one foot high. Nothing further is known concerning her history, beyond what is told by the inscription on this memorial.

"Ellonora Prochaska, known as one of the Lutzow Rifle Volunteers, by the name of Augustus Renz, born at Potzdam on the 11th March, 1785, received a fatal wound in the battle of Göhrde on the 15th September, 1813, died at Dannenberg on the 5th October, 1813. She fell exclaiming:—'Herr Lieutenant, I am a woman!'"

In 1869 a young man was received, by the express order of the King of Prussia, as a candidate for an ensign's commission into the second company of the first battalion of the 9th regiment, in Stargard, the same company in which his grandmother had served as a subaltern officer during the war of liberation against the French, and bravely won the Iron Cross and the Russian order of St. George. This lady—Augusta Frederica Krüger—was a native of Friedland, in Mecklenberg. Not content with offering, like many of her countrywomen, her trinkets and her flowing hair on the altar of patriotism, she entered the ranks as a volunteer, under the name of Lübeck, and distinguished herself by her intrepidity on many a hard-fought field. On October 23, 1815, she received her discharge, and her services were mentioned in this document in the most flattering terms. In January, 1816, being present, dressed in the garments of her own sex, at the festival of the Iron Cross, held at Berlin, she attracted the attention of a sub-officer of Lancers, named Karl Köhler, to whom she was married, in the garrison church of Berlin, on March 5, of the same year. The church was densely packed with spectators on the occasion, every one anxious to witness the marriage of two Prussian subaltern officers. The heroic bride appeared in a handsome silk gown, and wore on her breast the orders she had honourably won, which, with her short hair, were the only signs or symbols of her former military career.

Marshal Massena once related how, during an action between the French and Russians at Buezenghen, he observed a young soldier, apparently scarcely more than a child, who belonged to the French Light Artillery, defending himself bravely against several herculean Cossacks and Bavarians. This young artilleryman, whose horse had been slain by the thrust of a Cossack lance, displayed the most determined courage. "I immediately despatched an officer and some men to his assistance, but they arrived too late. Although the action had taken place on the borders of the wood and in front of the bridge, the artilleryman had alone withstood the attack of the small body of Cossacks and Bavarians whom the officers and men I had despatched put to flight. His body was covered with wounds inflicted by shots, lances, and swords. There were at least thirty. And do you know, Madame," asked the Marshal, "what the *young man* was?"

"A woman!"

"Yes, a woman, and a handsome woman too! Although she was so covered with blood that it was difficult to judge of her beauty. She had followed her lover to the army. The latter was a Captain of Artillery; she never left him, and when he was killed, defended like a lioness the remains of him she loved. She was a native of Paris, her name was Louise Belletz, and she was the daughter of a fringe-maker."

It was in 1812 that the Chicago Massacre took place. For more than a year before, the Indian tribes residing near the remote lakes and the sources of the Mississippi had displayed great hostility towards the pale-faces; though for a long time they did not venture to proceed to extremities. But after the declaration of war between the United States and Great Britain, on the 18th May, 1812, the savages came forward in great numbers as the allies of the British, and acted with their customary barbarity. One of their worst deeds was the Massacre of Chicago, August 15th, 1812.

The Fort of Chicago was commanded by Captain Heald. On the 7th August, he received despatches announcing that the Pottawatomie Indians had declared war against the United States, and commanding him to evacuate the place. He marched out on the 15th, accompanied by all the women and children, and had not proceeded very far before they were surrounded by overwhelming numbers of redskins. The Americans defended themselves with their usual bravery; and though hardly more than one to twenty, they sold their lives dearly.

Mrs. Heald, who was in the thick of the fight, received seven wounds. Her horse, a splendid animal, was prized by the Indians, who valued it far higher than its rider, and tried their best to avoid hurting it. A savage was in the act of tearing off Mrs. Heald's bonnet to scalp her, when one of the St. Joseph's tribe ransomed her for ten bottles of whiskey and a mule.

Mrs. Helm, wife of the officer second in command, fought bravely for her life. She was wounded slightly in the ankle, and had her horse shot under her. Being attacked by a young savage who aimed a blow at her head with his tomahawk, she sprang on one side, and the stroke fell on her shoulder, inflicting a severe wound. She seized him round the neck, and endeavoured to snatch his scalping-knife; but another Indian came up and dragged her away. The new-comer proved to be a friend. Plunging Mrs. Helm into the lake, he held her there, despite her struggles, till the firing was over.

After fighting with desperate valour, until only twenty-seven of them were left, the Americans were compelled to surrender. The wife of one of the soldiers, hearing of the tortures which the savages inflicted on their prisoners, resolved to die sooner than let herself be taken. When her companions had given up their arms, the Indians wished to capture this woman; but rejecting all their promises of kind treatment, she fought so desperately that she was literally cut to pieces.

Captain Helm, twice wounded, was sent with his wife and children to Mackinaw on the eastern coast of Michigan, and delivered as prisoners of war to the British general, who received them kindly, and sent them to Detroit. Lieutenant Helm, also wounded, was taken to St. Louis; where he was liberated through the entreaties of Mr. Forsyth, an Indian trader. Mrs. Helm was taken to Detroit, where she was exchanged, together with Captain and Mrs. Heald, some time after.

III.

Doña Maria de Jesus, Private in the Brazilian Army (War of the Reconcave)—Russian Female Soldiers—Juana de Areito (Civil Wars in Spain, 1834)—Anita Garibaldi—Appolonia Jagiello (Rebellions in Poland, 1846 and '48, and Vienna and Hungary, '48)—Bravery of the Croatian Women—Countess Helena St. ——, a Hungarian Patriot—Garde Mobile—Louisa Battistati (Milanese Revolution, 1848)—Fatima, a Turkish Commander (Russo-Turkish War)—Lady Paget (Attack on the Mamelon, June, 1855)—Miss Wheeler (Cawnpore Massacre)—Queen of Naples—Polish Insurrection—Mdlle. Pustowjtoff, Adjutant to Langievicz—Female Polish Chasseurs—Female Lieut.-Colonel in the Mexican Army—Civil War in America—Female Privates in the Potomac Army—Female Lieutenant and Privates in the Army of the West—Mrs. Clayton, Private in the Federal Army—Emily ——, Private in the Drum Corps of a Michigan Regiment—Female Confederates at Ringgold, Chattanooga—Mrs. Florence Bodwin—Female Mulatto Sergeant—Native Contingent in New Zealand—Herminia Manelli, Corporal of Bersaglieri (Battle of Custozza, 1866)—Lopez's Amazons—Cretan Amazons—Women of Montenegro—Female Brigands—German Order to Reward Courage in Women—Franco-Prussian War—Minna Hänsel's Amazon Corps.

SINCE the first French Revolution, monarchs have not always sat easily upon their thrones. They fancied they had cut down the Tree of Liberty after the downfall of Napoleon, and that it would never grow up again; but in a very short time it brought forth new branches, and has since borne fruit in a way which the most sanguine Republican of olden times would scarcely have ventured to predict. Since the battle of Waterloo, Europe and America—even parts of Asia and Africa—have been convulsed by rebellions, civil wars, and revolutions, which have often shaken the world to its centre. The peoples learnt to hate their rulers; and one nation after another, catching the revolutionary fire from the smouldering brand half stamped out in France, rose in rebellion against the monarch who refused them immediate enfranchisement. Again and again have the nations been compelled by force of arms to submit; but they rise again whenever they fancy they see a favourable opportunity. Thus it happened that almost every war, fought in Europe or America since Waterloo up to some ten years since, had its origin in the same cause—the struggles of nations to cast off their rulers.

Amongst those states which took the initiative in raising the standard of revolt, the South American colonies of Spain and Portugal were foremost. Brazil declared its independence in 1821, and elected Don Pedro, the Crown Prince of Portugal, to be Emperor. The latter had a hard struggle to maintain his throne against not only the Portuguese troops, but against the Republicans, who composed a large party in Brazil. His emissaries were despatched all over the country, to the most distant plantations, to raise recruits for the Imperial Army. One of these messengers arrived one day at the farm-house of Gonzalez de Almeida, a Portuguese settler in the parish of San José, on the Rio de Pax. The patriot was invited to dinner; and, mindful of his object, he endeavoured to enlist the sympathies of his host for Don Pedro. Almeida listened very attentively; but it awakened no feelings of patriotism in his breast. He was old, and could not join the army himself, nor had he a son to give.

"As to giving a slave," added he, "what interest would a slave have in fighting for the independence of Brazil?"

But though Almeida had no sons, he had two daughters. One of them, Doña Maria de Jesus, was desirous, for many reasons, to leave home and seek employment elsewhere. Her father had married again, and the step-mother and her young children made home exceedingly uncomfortable for Maria. She was much excited by the patriot's words; "So that at last," she said, " I felt my heart burning in my breast!"

She stole from the house, and went to that of her married sister. After recapitulating the stranger's discourse, she expressed a wish that she were a man and could join the Imperial standard.

"Nay," said her sister. "If I had not a husband and child, for one half of what you say, I would join the ranks of the emperor."

This decided the wavering resolution of Doña Maria. Her sister supplied her with a suit of clothes belonging to the husband, so Maria took the opportunity, as her father was going to Cachoeira, about forty leagues distant, to dispose of some cotton, to ride after him; not close enough to be seen, but sufficiently near for protection. When in sight of Cachoeira, she halted; and going a little way from the road, dressed herself in male attire.

She entered the town on a Friday, and by the following Sunday she had enlisted in an artillery regiment, and had already mounted guard. She was, however, too slight for the heavy duties of an artilleryman; so she exchanged into an infantry corps, in which she remained till the close of the war.

Her real sex was not even suspected till Almeida applied to the commanding officer of her regiment. In the summer of 1823 she was sent with despatches to Rio Janeiro, and there presented to Don Pedro, who gave her an ensign's commission and the Order of the Cross—the latter of which he himself placed upon her jacket.

Maria Graham in her "Journal of a Voyage to Brazil," gives, as one of the illustrations, Maria de Jesus in her uniform. "Her dress," says this traveller, " is that of a soldier of one of the emperor's battalions, with the addition of a tartan kilt, which she told me she had adopted from a picture representing a Highlander, as the most feminine military dress. What would the Gordons and Macdonalds say to this? The 'garb of old Gaul' chosen as a womanish attire!" This lady further says that Maria, though clever, was almost totally uneducated; " she might have been a remarkable person. She is not particularly masculine in her appearance, and her manners are gentle and cheerful."

In a census of the population of St. Petersburg, published about 1829, there appears the following curious item :—

"SOLDIERS AND SUBALTERNS.

Men.	Women.	Total.
46,076	9,975	56,051."

When the civil war broke out in Spain, in 1634, the town of Eybar, in the province of Guipuzcoa, being attacked by Zabala, the Carlist general, several women and girls assisted the Christino troops in its defence. One of these brave girls, Juana de Anito, at this time barely fifteen, was married six years later to Don Eulogio Barbero Quintero, a young officer in the Spanish Army. In 1840 he became mixed up in a conspiracy against the Government; and on the failure of the plot, attempted to escape into France. He was intercepted on his road, and imprisoned in the citadel of San Sebastian. Directly Juana heard of his capture she resolved to effect his escape; which she accomplished in Nov. 1841, by exchanging clothes with him. Don Eulogio succeeded in reaching the French frontier; but the courage and devotion of his young wife did not avert the wrath of the Spanish Regent, by whose orders she was condemned to imprisonment for life.

It was whilst fighting in Brazil as a rebel against the Imperial Government that Garibaldi first met his beloved wife, Anita. She was a Brazilian by birth, and possessed all the beauty of her countrywomen. Her complexion was a clear olive, set off by piercing black eyes, her figure tall and commanding. She was a fit companion for the brave Garibaldi; being to the full as courageous as he. The general himself said that his wife took part in battle as " an amusement " and " a simple variation to the monotony of camp-life."

Anita accompanied her husband in all his expeditions both on shore and at sea. Ably did she second him in the struggle for Brazilian freedom. Shortly after marriage they were one day at sea, when the Imperial fleet hove in sight, and bore down upon them. Garibaldi entreated his bride to land, and remain on shore whilst the engagement lasted; but she firmly refused, and not only remained during the action, but took a very leading share in it. One of the sailors fell dead at her feet; she snatched up his carbine, and kept up a constant fire on the Brazilians for several hours.

When the battle was at its height, Anita was standing on deck, waving a sword over her head, encouraging the men to resist bravely. Suddenly she was struck down by the wind of a cannon-ball, which killed two men close by. Garibaldi rushed forward, expecting to find that life was extinct; but to his astonishment and delight she rose up unhurt. Again he entreated her to go below, and remain there till the fighting was over.

"Yes," said Anita. "I will go below; but only to drive out the cowards who are skulking there."

And running down the hatchway, she speedily reappeared, driving before her three men who had gone below to escape the storm.

Anita was also present, on horseback, in a battle fought at a place called Coritibani, where the Garibaldians, numbering scarcely eighty men, half of whom were infantry, were attacked by a large body of Brazilian cavalry. She was not satisfied with being a mere spectator; knowing that the rebels, as they kept up a constant fire, would soon exhaust their amunition, she went to the baggage-waggons to see that the men were properly supplied with cartridges. She had not been there very long before the baggage-train was attacked by twenty or thirty Brazilian horsemen. Anita was a good rider, and could have saved herself; but she preferred to remain on the spot, encouraging the Garibaldians.

The Brazilians were victorious in this battle; Anita surrounded on every side, received orders to yield. Clapping spurs to her horse, she dashed through the midst of her foes. Several shots were fired after her; one, a pistol shot, went through her hat, cutting off a lock of hair, while another pierced her horse's head. The animal fell heavily to the ground, flinging her with violence from the saddle. Before she could recover her feet, the Brazilian troopers had made her prisoner.

Anita believed that her husband had been killed; so the Brazilian colonel gave her permission to search the battle-field for his body. She looked through the corpses again and again for several hours, and at last came to the conclusion that Garibaldi still lived, and she determined to rejoin him. That night, when the Brazilians had retired to rest, and when even the sentry began to nod, she succeeded in escaping to a farmhouse a quarter of a mile distant; where she seized a horse, and plunged into the forest, in the direction which she believed the Garibaldians to have taken.

For more than a week, Anita Garibaldi wandered alone amidst the almost impenetrable wilds of the dense Brazilian forests, without food, and exposed to the hourly chances of capture. More than once she was pursued by the enemy placed in ambush at various points. One stormy night, four horsemen, who were stationed at a ford of the river Canoas, believing her to be a phantom, fled in terror. Anita plunged boldly into the stream; and, although it was five hundred yards broad, and swollen by the mountain rivulets till it had assumed the aspect of a roaring cataract, she succeeded, holding on by her horse's mane, in reaching the opposite shore, amidst a shower of bullets from the Brazilians, who had found out their mistake.

After enduring for eight days every kind of danger and privation, she overtook the Garibaldians, and rejoined her husband.

"Yes, yes, gentlemen," added Garibaldi, when he related this anecdote, "my wife is valiant."

There are many more of these anecdotes related concerning the extraordinary bravery of Anita. She afterwards accompanied her husband on his return to Italy, in 1848, and was with him during the insurrection of Lombardy against Austria. In the following year she attended him throughout the siege of Rome. After the fall of the Eternal City in 1849, when Garibaldi was escaping to Venice, Anita, worn out by long suffering, died at Mandriole, a small village in the marshes of Ravenna.

Apollonia Jagiello, a Polish heroine, who acquired no little celebrity for her bravery during the insurrections of '46 and '48, was born in Lithuania, in 1825. She was educated at Cracow, in which city she passed her early life; sometimes changing for a few weeks to Warsaw or Vienna. In 1846 the insurrection broke out in the former city. Apollonia was, at this time, rather more than twenty, of medium height, with a graceful and slender figure. She was a brunette, with big black eyes, and a profusion of dark hair. Her arms and hands, which were more than once admired by those who saw her, were beautiful, and delicately formed. Although her lips were usually compressed, with a resolute expression of one who was not easily daunted, yet she could also smile most sweetly. "In that," says the *National Era* (an American journal), "the woman comes out; it is arch, soft and winning—a rare and indescribable smile. Her manner," adds this paper, "is simple and engaging. Her voice is now gentle or mirthful, now earnest and passionate—sometimes it sounds like the utterance of some quiet home lyre, and sometimes startles you with a decided ring of the steel."

Apollonia, inspired by that enthusiastic love for

her country, which we so often find amongst Polish girls, joined the national army; and, throughout the struggle, which lasted only two or three months, was always found wherever danger was greatest. Mounted on horseback, she was one of those patriots who planted the White Eagle and the flag of freedom on the Castle and Palace of Cracow. She also formed one of that gallant little band which fought the battle near Podgorze against an army ten times their strength.

When the insurrection was suppressed, Madlle. Jagiello, resuming her own attire, remained in Cracow for several weeks without detection. She then removed to Warsaw, where she stayed until the year 1848, the Year of Revolutions. Directly the Cracovians took up arms, she joined their ranks, and displayed the same courage which she had shown two years previously.

The insurrection of '48 proved, if possible, a greater failure than the first. Apollonia fled from Cracow, and reached Vienna just in time to take share in the skirmish of the Faubourg Widen. She remained here only a few days, her object being to join the Hungarian insurgents under Kossuth. With the assistance of some friends she succeeded in reaching Presburg; whence, disguised as a peasant, she was conveyed to the village of St. Paul by those unfortunate country-folks who were compelled to carry provisions for the Austrian army. Crossing that part of the country occupied by the German troops, she reached the Hungarian camp, near the village of Ezneszey, on the 15th August, 1848. This was immediately before the battle fought here, in which the Austrians were defeated, and General Wist slain. Apollonia took part in this battle as a volunteer; but such was her courage that the Hungarian general presented her with a lieutenant's commission.

Apollonia, on the urgent solicitation of all, undertook the superintendence of the hospital at Comorn. This post she resigned for a while to join as a volunteer in the expedition of twelve thousand men, commanded by General Klapka, who captured Raab. Returning to Comorn, the heroine resumed her hospital duties, and remained there until the fortress surrendered.

In December, 1849, in company with Governor Ladislaus Ujhazy and his family, Apollonia Jagiello sailed to the United States, where they received an enthusiastic welcome. Here she continued to show that hatred of tyrants for which she had ever been distinguished. One day, when she was at Washington, an album was handed to her, with the request that she would add her autograph to those it already contained. She took it with a smile, but it chanced that on the very page at which she opened, the signature of M. Bodisco, the Russian ambassador, figured prominently. Flinging the album from her, with flashing eyes, she declared that her name should never appear in the same book with " the tool of a tyrant."

While the hatred of Austria was felt by all throughout Hungary, Croatia and Sclavonia were actuated, on the contrary, by feelings of the deepest loyalty to the house of Hapsburg. Baron W., who published his adventures under the title of "Scenes of the Civil War in Hungary in 1848-9, with the personal adventures of an Austrian officer, etc.," declares that the Croatians joined the Imperial standard by thousands; even the women, moved by an ardent and loyal courage, aided in defending the frontiers against the Bosnians, who, excited by the emissaries of Kossuth, took every opportunity for raids and invasions over the border. While the men were flocking to the banners of Jellachich, the ban of Croatia, their wives and daughters took up arms and repaired to the chain of posts on the Turkish boundary, " that all the men might be able to take the field; and such an eight days' duty as these frontier posts," he adds, " is no trifle, and requires not a little firmness. Old, half-invalided frontier subalterns, incapacitated for taking the field, were the commandants; young, many of them handsome, females composed their troops. " By my faith ! " exclaims the Baron, "I should have no objection to be the commander of such a corps of Ottochan females myself!"

Numbers of Croatian and Sclavonian women accompanied the Austrian army into Germany and Italy. "We had," says the same author, "wives and daughters of frontier soldiers with us in Peschiera and on the march through Hungary, who equalled the men in the endurance of fatigue, and displayed undaunted courage in battle. In Hungary we had with us a young Croatian, the daughter of an old Seressan, who was as daring a rider as the best hussar, and more than once fearlessly joined the men in the charge. A Hungarian *jurat* gave her in an action a cut on the left cheek, which she returned with a severe blow on the arm, seized the bridle of his horse, and took him prisoner. This horse, a grey stallion, she ever afterwards rode, and refused to sell, though I offered her forty ducats for him."

The Countess Helene St——, a Hungarian patriot, was the sister of an old comrade of Baron W. The brother, who owned a magnificent estate, was a Magyar to the very core; and directly the insurrection broke out, he took up arms, and fell bravely fighting for his country in February, 1849. His dying agonies were soothed by an unexpected meeting with his early friend, the Baron.

Helene joined the insurgents soon after her brother

left home, and served as aide-de-camp to his maternal uncle, who commanded a considerable Magyar corps. One cold, moonlight night, a few days after the death of the count, the author of the "Adventures" discovered the corpse of this beautiful girl, dressed in the military uniform of a Hungarian soldier, stretched out at the foot of a tree, her life's blood crimsoning the white snow.

"Forcibly mustering my spirits," says he, "I ordered my men to carry the body to the fire. There we examined it more closely, and with extreme anxiety I sought to ascertain whether there was any hope left of reviving her. Vain hope! It was several hours since her spirit had departed; the ball of one of our riflemen had gone through her heart. From the small red wound blood was still oozing in a single drop, which I carefully caught in my handkerchief to be preserved as a relic.

"My only consolation was that the deceased could not have suffered long; that she must have expired the very moment she was struck. Those pure, noble, still wondrous beautiful features; on her brow dwelt peace and composure, and the lips almost smiled. There she lay, as if in tranquil slumber, and yet those eyes were never more to open—those lips never more to utter noble sentiments or words of kindness.

"My hussars were visibly affected, and thought it

a pity that one so young and so beautiful should die so early. Many of them who had been with me on our first march through Hungary for two days together at St——'s mansion, instantly recognised Helene, and doubly lamented her death, because she had shown such kindness to them."

They dug a deep grave beneath the frozen snow. "The corpse, in full uniform; the *holpack*, with plume of glistening heron's feathers on her head, the light Turkish sabre by her side, was then carefully wrapped in a clean large blanket which we had with us, and so deposited in the grave, which we filled up again with earth. Then regardless of caution, I had a full salute fired with pistols over the grave. I have preserved a small gold ring and a lock of her hair for a memorial."

The Baron, it should be added, plainly tells the reader that he was very nearly, if not quite, over head and ears in love with the beautiful Helene.

One of the hussars, who could do carpenter's work, made a cross of two young, white maple trees, which was placed over the heroine's grave.

The Garde Mobile (which, as an extra battalion to the National Guard, did good service to the people in '48,) when it was disbanded, proved to be half composed of Parisian women and girls.

Louisa Battistati, a heroine of the Lombardian Revolution, was a native of Stradella, in Sardinia, and a mantua-maker by trade. She was dwelling in Milan, following this business, when the five days' Revolution broke out. On Sunday, the 10th March, 1848, Louisa attacked and disarmed an Austrian cavalry soldier, although he carried a carbine. At the head of a valiant band of young women, she now took up her station at the Poppietti bridge, and defended it all through the 20th, the 21st and the 22nd. At every shot from her musket a Croat fell dead.

In June, 1853, the war between Russia and Turkey broke out. The Turkish government, to swell the ranks of the army, were obliged to beat up for recruits among the semi-barbarous tribes of Asia Minor. The chief of one of the wild tribes in the Cilician mountains having been imprisoned by order of the Sultan, his wife, Fatima, a little old woman, about sixty years of age, with a dark complexion, who governed during his absence, exercising the double duty of Queen and Prophetess, raised three hundred of her best horsemen and led them to the Allied Camp at Scutari, in the summer of 1854. Her appearance created no little sensation amongst English and French. There was very little of the Amazon in her personal appearance, though she bestrode her steed like a trooper, and wore a costume intended to represent the military dress of a chieftain. She was attended by two handmaids, also in male attire.

Fatima, apprehensive that her entreaties for the release of her husband would prove insufficient to move the Sultan, thought the best means of propitiating the Turkish Government was to lead a few hundreds of her bravest warriors to fight the frozen Russ. The pay for her troops was to be eighty piastres a month, besides tooth and stirrup money in every village through which they should pass.

When the Allies were storming the Mamelon in June, 1855, Lady Paget (wife of Lord George, and daughter of General Sir Arthur Paget, brother of the famous Marquis of Anglesey) was present on the field, at a short distance from the scene of action. General Pennefather went up to the dead body of a Russian officer, and cut a medal off his coat. He then pinned the medal on Lady Paget's shawl, paying her a handsome compliment to the effect that she deserved a medal as much as any one present.

Most people can remember the fortitude and courage displayed by the British ladies at Cawnpore, Lucknow, and other Indian cities during the terrible Mutiny. Ladies, some of them mere girls, delicately nurtured, unused to hardships of any kind, endured without a murmur, the most heartrending privations ; and so far from giving way to useless repinings or sinking into apathy, they tried in every way to cheer up their brave defenders. They bore provisions and ammunition to the soldiers, loaded the rifles, and more than once took their turn in mounting guard and firing on the rebels.

The heroine of Cawnpore, Miss Wheeler, was one of the prisoners captured by the notorious Nana Sahib on the 26th June, 1857, and all who survived the terrible Massacre bore witness to her unflinching courage. She is said to have shot five Sepoys with a revolver; that she was then taken away by a sowar (trooper) to his hut, when she snatched his sabre, cut off his head, and flung herself down a well. An ayah, belonging to an English family, stated that it was in the hut, after killing the sowar, that she shot the five Sepoys.

The romantic conquest of Naples and Sicily, by General Garibaldi in 1860, has already melted into the past and become an almost distant event in European history. It was said at the time that if Francis II. had possessed a particle of the military courage of his Queen, it would have been easy for him with his trained battalions to have captured or dispersed the handful of Garibaldian volunteers. When Bombino had taken refuge in Gaeta, the great stronghold of Southern Italy, he fancied himself secure from the attacks of the foe; but the Sardinian troops were soon battering the walls with long-range guns, and all the appliances necessary for a modern siege.

Amongst the besieged, Queen Marie Sophie Amelie was the only leader who encouraged the soldiers to make a brave defence. Standing on the ramparts of Gaeta, she incited the Neapolitan troops to shed the last drop of their blood for the Bourbon cause. Doubtless there was much exaggeration in those marvellous anecdotes published in the newspapers of the time relating deeds of Amazonian valour performed by the Queen; but it is certain that she acted the part of King, while her cowardly husband hid away in the darkness and security of bomb-proof galleries. In December, 1860, and January, 1861, it was remarked by the troops of Cialdini that every morning, at a particular hour, the fire of the Neapolitan batteries slackened for a short time; re-commencing, however, with renewed vigour. They soon learned that the Queen, dressed in Calabrian costume, visited a particular battery (named after herself the "Queen's Battery") every morning, sometimes on horseback, but generally in a coach; and would assist in the firing of the heavy guns. The artillerymen were ready to sacrifice their lives in the service of their beautiful and courageous

Queen, while they heartily despised the contemptible Francis.

The chief heroine of the last Polish insurrection (1862-3-4) was Madlle. Pustowjtoff, or, as some have written it, Pustovoydova, aide-de-camp and Adjutant to General Langievicz, the Dictator. When the ill-starred rebellion was at its height cartes-de-visite of the heroine, in the costume of a Polish officer, were displayed in the shop-windows of the great European and American cities, side by side with all the public celebrities of the day. She was decidedly pretty, though rather childish looking: her features were good, and she had a profusion of fair hair.

Though her family and her proclivities were essentially Polish, Madlle Pustowjtoff was not a native of the country, but was born in Russia of a Polish mother. When the insurrection broke out, she escaped from a convent where she had been placed (probably by her parents) and joined Langievicz, who almost immediately appointed her to be one of his aides. She was present in numberless battles and skirmishes between the Russians and Poles; and finally accompanied Langievicz in his precipitate—some say cowardly—flight into Galicia, where, being arrested by the Austrian authorities, the fugitives were imprisoned. Madlle.

Pustowjtoff was afterwards released on parole, though she was requested not to quit Galicia. In November, 1863, she exchanged the profession of arms for the occupation of companion to a lady in that country; but after the release of Langievicz and his followers by the Austrian Government in the summer of 1865, she resigned this employment, and travelled westwards.

There was many another Polish heroine as brave though not so famous as the female Adjutant. When national liberty is at stake, there will always be found women as well as men ready to arm in its defence; and the women of Poland have ever been remarked for more than ordinary patriotism. A writer in *Fraser's Magazine* for December, 1863, speaking of the part taken by the Polish women in the struggles with Russia, relates the following anecdotes of female courage :—

"The following incident of the active heroism of the Polish women, was told me by an officer who had commanded a detachment of cavalry in Lithuania in the early days of the insurrection :—

"One day about twenty of his Cossacks surrounded the house of a lady, living in a retired part of the country, whose daughter was the betrothed of one of the chiefs of bands known to be in the neighbourhood. At that very moment he and several other leaders were in the house, consulting with the two ladies over their plans. Alarmed by the arrival of the Cossacks, the men hastened to escape from the back windows, and fled to the woods; the two women actually protecting their retreat by keeping up a fire from their pistols from the front. When the Cossacks at last forced their way into the house, they found only the two women, whom they do not seem to have molested, but contented themselves, after their manner, with filling their pockets with all the portable valuables within reach. On retiring, they pitched their horses a short distance off, yet in sight of the house. Presently the young girl was seen to come out, and proceed to the stables, from which she soon again came forth, mounted, when she set off in the direction her lover had taken. One of the Cossacks, having a sorry beast of his own, and admiring that which the girl rode, galloped after her, took hold of her bridle, and, as good-humouredly as his rough nature allowed, proposed an exchange, observing that as she was going to join the band, she had no need of such a good horse. The reply was a bullet from her revolver which sent the Cossack reeling from his saddle. Meanwhile his companions, who had followed him, had come up, and seeing the fate of their comrade, surrounded her. The intrepid girl then snapped her pistol at one after the other, and when all the chambers of this one were discharged, flung the empty weapon at the head of the nearest, knocking him from his horse, and immediately drew forth a second. This was too much for the politeness of the Cossacks, of whom three or four were already on the ground; they lifted the poor girl completely off her horse on the points of their lances, and so she perished.

"As a further example," continues this writer, "I will translate an extract from a private letter lately received from an officer serving in the kingdom of Poland:—'Yesterday,' says the officer who wrote it, 'we defeated a band and took nineteen prisoners, one of whom was a woman. There were altogether seven of them belonging to that band, but we do not as yet know if the others were killed or escaped. All the women, our prisoner tells us, were dressed as *chasseurs*, wearing the same uniform of coarse cloth as the men, only without the red epaulette. Their caps, such as are worn by all the Confederates, were coquettishly made, and decorated with a white ostrich feather. We captured her by the merest chance. She was a girl from Cracow, finely built, with broad shoulders, and muscular hand and arm, which showed she had been used to gymnastic exercises, while her weather-beaten complexion proved she must have belonged to the band for some length of time. Her features, without being pretty, were regular and agreeable. On our asking her reasons for serving with the band, she confessed she had followed her lover to the woods, adding that, when he was killed, she would have gone back home, but was prevented by her comrades. Somebody asking if she had not served as aide-de-camp to C—(the chief of another band), she blushed deeply, and indignantly denied the imputation. After this reply, she was very haughty and retired for a time; but, seeing that we were all respectful to her, she gradually became more at home with us and confiding in her conversation. As she had lost her boots, and was bare-footed, we furnished her with a pair of our long boots and some stockings, for which the poor girl was very thankful. The next day she was released and sent home, her male companions being forwarded on to Warsaw.'"

During the war between France and Mexico, several women and girls were discovered fighting in the ranks of Juarez. One of them, a young Indian, aged twenty-two, enlisted with her husband, in the regiment of Zacatócas. She fought so bravely as to speedily gain her epaulettes. Her husband was slain; but the widow remained in the regiment, where her daring courage soon not only procured the esteem of her superior officers, but caused the Mexican generals to promote her to the rank of lieutenant-colonel, May 5th, 1862. When the French captured

Puebla, in the summer of 1863, she was made prisoner, and sent to Vera Cruz; whence she embarked in the "Rhône" steam transport for France. During the voyage, though a prisoner, she was treated with all the respect due to a superior officer. She arrived in France in August, 1863, and was seen by many persons, who described the female colonel as rather good-looking, but somewhat unfeminine in outward carriage and bearing.

If we may believe Transatlantic newspapers, the Civil War in America was more productive of female warriors than almost any conflict since the days of the Amazons. The ranks of both Federals and Confederates, from the very commencement of the great struggle, were swelled by numbers of women, who, for various reasons, chose to risk their lives under the Stars and Stripes, or the Stars and Bars. In the summer of 1864, it was said that upwards of one hundred and fifty women were known to be serving in the Army of the Potomac. It was generally supposed that these women had been in collusion with an equal number of men who had been examined by the surgeons; after which the fair ones substituted themselves, and went to the seat of war. More than seventy of the valiant *demoiselles* were, when their sex became known, acting as officers' servants.

Early in May, 1863, a Pennsylvania girl was discovered serving in one of the regiments in the Federal Army of the West, to which she had belonged for ten months. She said that there were many females in the ranks of this army, and one female lieutenant. She had herself, she declared, assisted in burying three female soldiers whose sex was unknown to any but her.

Mrs. Francis L. Clayton, another female Federal, enlisted in 1861, in company with her husband at St. Paul, Minnesota. The husband and wife fought together, side by side, in eighteen battles, till the former was slain in the engagement of Stone River. After his death, the wife did not care to remain any longer in the service, so she went to the general, and told him she was a woman, and was at once discharged. She then returned to Maine. During her military career, Mrs. Clayton was wounded three times, and once was made prisoner.

The following story, "strange if true," appeared in the *Brooklyn* (New York) *Times*, in October, 1863, just after the battle of Chattanooga :—

"About a twelvemonth since, when disaster everywhere overtook the Union arms, and our gallant sons were falling fast under the marvellous sword of rebellion, a young lady, scarce nineteen, from an academy in a sister State, conceived the idea that she was destined by Providence to lead our armies to victory, and our nation through successful war. It was at first thought by her parents—a highly respectable family in Willoughby-street—that her mind was weakened simply by reading continual accounts of reverses to our arms, and they treated her as a sick child. This only had the effect of making her more demonstrative, and her enthusiastic declaration and apparent sincerity gave the family great anxiety. Dr. B. was consulted, the minister was spoken to, friends advised, family meetings held, interviews with the young lady and her former companions in the academy were frequent, but nothing could shake the feeling which possessed her. It was finally resolved to take her to Michigan. An old maiden aunt accompanied the fair enthusiast, and for weeks Anne Arbour became their home. But travel had no effect upon the girl. The stern command of her aunt alone prevented her from making her way to Washington to solicit an interview with the President for the purpose of getting command of the United States Army. Finally it was found necessary to restrain her from seeing any one but her own family, and her private parlour became her prison. To a high-spirited girl that would be unendurable at any time, but to a young lady filled with such an hallucination it was worse than death. She resolved to elude her friends, and succeeded,—leaving them clandestinely,—and, although the most distinguished detectives of the east and west were employed to find her whereabouts, it was unavailing. None could conjecture her hiding-place. This was last April. She was mourned as lost, the habiliments of mourning were assumed by her grief-stricken parents, and a suicide's grave was assumed to be hers. But it was not so. The infatuated girl, finding no sympathy among her friends, resolved to enter the army, disguised as a drummer boy, dreaming, poor girl, that her destiny would be worked out by such a mode. She joined the drum-corps of a Michigan regiment at Detroit, her sex known only to herself, and succeeded in getting with her regiment to the Army of the Cumberland. How the poor girl survived the hardships of the Kentucky campaign, when strong men fell in numbers, must for ever remain a mystery. The regiment to which she was attached had a place in the division of the gallant Van Cleve, and, during the bloody battle of last Sunday, the fair girl fell, pierced in the left side with a Minié ball, and, when borne to the surgeon's tent, her sex was discovered. She was told by the surgeon that her wound was mortal, and advised to give her name, that her family might be informed of her fate. This she finally, though reluctantly, consented to do, and the colonel of the regiment, suffering himself from a painful wound, became interested in her behalf, and prevailed upon her to let him send a despatch to her father. Here, then, is a short incident of the war, which might read like romance, but to the unhappy family which are now bowed down by grief, romance loses its attraction, and the actual sad, eventful history of poor Emily —— will be a family record for generations to come."

In December, 1863, the correspondent of the *Cincinnati Times*, describing a skirmish between the Federals and a detachment of General Bragg's army at Ringgold, near Chattanooga, says " Several of the fair sex were in the Confederate ranks, and certainly conducted themselves with a great deal of courage. We make no reflection on their taste in entering the ranks with negroes and greasy greybacks. Rebellion now needs every aid on the earth above or in the caverns under it."

At Timonsville, S.C., is the grave of Mrs. Florence Bodwin, of Philadelphia, Pa. She was a member of a Federal regiment, and as such, being dressed as a soldier, her sex was not discovered until after her death.

The following anecdote went the round of the papers in October, 1865, though the event chronicled must have taken place some time previously, doubtless before the close of the war :—

" At Theresina, a mulatto girl, nineteen years old, cut her hair, bandaged her bosom, and dressed as a man, went to the President to offer herself as a volunteer. The President detected her sex, and supposed at first that she was mad, or had taken this plan to accompany a lover; but finding that she was really actuated by patriotism, he accepted her, and appointed her second sergeant, and she does all the duties of her post, dressed in the proper uniform."

The Maori War in New Zealand, like the conflicts between the Red Skins and the Pale Faces in North America, gave many opportunities for the wives and daughters of settlers to play the heroine. Some of the native women, too, displayed great prowess, both for and against the English. A correspondent of the *Irish Times*, writing from Wanganui, under date of the 7th January, 1866, in describing the native contingent (a force recruited from the Wanganui River Tribes) to which he was Assistant Surgeon, says "Numbers of women accompany us, who generally carry the baggage of the men. This is not their only use in campaigning. They fight, and fight well, carrying their gun and tomahawk."

During the Austro-Italian war of 1866, a Florence journal related that, after the battle of Custozza (June 27th), a surgeon of the Italian army discovered among the wounded a young corporal of Bersaglieri still alive, notwithstanding three severe injuries in the neck, left arm, and right leg. When about to dress those wounds the surgeon perceived that the sufferer was a young woman, who then declared her name to be Herminia Manelli, and her age twenty. Just before the opening of the campaign her brother, who was a corporal of Bersaglieri, had fallen ill, and returned home to his family until his recovery. The sister, whose parents had previously had some difficulty in preventing from joining the Garibaldians, took advantage of that circumstance, and, cutting short her hair, dressed herself in her brother's uniform, and joined his regiment, her resemblance to him enabling her to pass unnoticed. Four hours later her regiment was engaged, and she was wounded on the field of battle. After the discovery of her sex by the surgeon she was taken to Florence, where she died a few days later.

In the summer of 1868, there was a great deal of talk about an army of women which had just been raised by the savage Lopez, Dictator of Paraguay. A correspondent writing from Buenos Ayres under date May 14th, says:—

"An army of women confronts the allies! Lopez has enrolled the Amazons of Paraguay, and we have entered upon what may be called for the sake of distinction—the petticoat campaign? Brigadier-

General Eliza Lynch commands the main body of the female army, which is encamped midway between the pass of the river and a small inland town. On the road to Villa Rica her right wing, under Mrs. Captain Herrero, has deployed to the left a little, to hang on the allies should they assail the position of Tebiquary, held by Mrs. Lieutenant Colonel Margaret Fereira and her fair brigade of womankind. Can 'stern-visaged Mars' prove unpropitious? ... According to authentic accounts, relays of women and girls are constantly at the head-quarters of the feminine commander-in-chief to whom has been entrusted the guerilla portion of the campaign."

The Brazilian journals were of course indignant at what they termed an outrage on civilization, and alternately sneered and railed at Lopez's petticoat *corps d'armée*. Very little was afterwards heard of these Amazons. Since their first formation, with the exception of a few stray anecdotes related by travellers and adventurers returning to the States or to this country, absolutely nothing transpired concerning the movements of this female army.

Again we meet with female warriors in the struggle between Crete and Turkey. " Whether they have been effectual defenders of their country," says a writer in a newspaper eleven years ago, "or whether their enthusiasm decreased before the stern necessity of a camp, is hardly known, for very little intelligence comes from the mountains of Crete." However, in January, 1869, a body of about fifty Cretan Amazons, in uniform, was seen at Michali, practising shooting with carbines at a mark. They were, it is said, very good shots, and had been organised into a regular corps, with a regimental flag, which was carried by a *religieuse* who had turned Amazon.

The Philo-Cretan Committee recognised the patriotism of these Lakkoite damsels, by providing them with arms (consisting of a rifle of the English pattern with a sword-bayonet) and handsome uniforms similar to those worn by the Palikares. This costume included the fez, a corset embroidered in gold and silver, a short, piquant half-sleeved jacket, a white petticoat and "continuations," and the most charmingly neat buckskin gaiters. A cartridge-box hung to the belt, while a havresack depended from the shoulders. Picturesque sketches of these heroines, in uniform, appeared in the French and English journals of January, '69.

But while a few of the Cretan women have proved themselves heroines, bravery has been the character of those of Montenegro for more than half a century. War against the Mussulman is the object, the engrossing passion of nearly every Montenegrin—men, women, and children, cripples even, rush to the fight with enthusiasm. In truth, the Turkish Government has never been able thoroughly to subdue the Black Mountain. Women accompany their male relatives in all their expeditions against the infidels, wives are ever ready to seize up the yataghan and pistols of a slain husband, and avenge his death. Various heroic ballads have been sung or recited from time to time in the fastnesses of the Tsernogora relating the martial deeds of some valiant widow who has slain Turkish Agas, captured or dispersed, single-handed, whole companies of the foe, or in other ways distinguished their military courage and their hatred of the Moslem.

A singular incident is alleged to have taken place some nine years since on the occasion of a marriage before the chief authorities in Algeria. The official required the consent of the bride's mother, and asked if she was present. A sonorous bass voice answered "Yes." The Mayor looked up and saw a tall soldier before him. "That is well," said he. "Let the mother come here. Her consent and signature are necessary." To the astonishment of all present, the soldier approached the Mayor with long strides, saluted military fashion, and said—"You ask for the mother of the bride. She stands before you." "Very well, sir," replied the Mayor. "Then stand back. I can take no proxy. I must see the mother

—the mother, I tell you." "And I repeat that she stands before you," rejoined the soldier. "My name is Maria L——. I have been thirty-six years in the service. I have been through several campaigns, and obtained the rank of sergeant. Here are my papers—the permission to wear uniform, and my nomination as sergeant-major." The mayor carefully examined the documents, and found them perfectly correct. There was nothing to be done but to complete the marriage of the young couple. The mother bestowed her blessing fervently with her deep bass voice in a manner which impressed all present, but the company were "more startled than touched."

The Brigand chiefs of Southern Italy are the last representatives of the Condottieri who ravaged the land in olden times. But so far from improving with the march of intellect and growing more civilized, the bandits of our days would seem to have very decidedly retrograded as regards the more polite arts of life; indeed, they are nothing but savage beasts, who can handle the carbine or the dagger, and have the passions of avarice and the thirst for gold added to the reckless cruelty of the tiger. These ferocious brigands are almost invariably accompanied in their adventurous journey through life by some beautiful fiend, either the wife or the mistress of the redoubtable chief. These women are often the most abandoned and worthless of their sex, without even the virtue of mercy—the tigress is not uncommonly worse than the tiger.

Amongst those brigand captains who, though almost unknown in Western Europe, have earned a terrible renown in the South of Italy, none was more feared and respected some seventeen or eighteen years ago than Monaco. His deeds of violence and daring audacity rendered him famous throughout the Neapolitan provinces. His wife, Maria Oliveiro, a remarkably handsome woman (about twenty years old in 1864), was his constant companion in all his marauding expeditions. She was unmistakably brave, but her nature was so ruthless that the sight of blood rendered her half mad. Monaco was at last slain in a desperate encounter with the Italian troops near Rossano. Maria was severely wounded; but without losing her courage or presence of mind, she planted one knee firmly on her husband's corpse, and continued to load and fire with extreme rapidity, exciting the admiration even of her opponents. At last she received a severe wound in the leg, and was made prisoner. She was tried by court-martial at Cattanzaro, and condemned to be shot; but this sentence was commuted to thirty years' penal servitude, and she had not been very long in gaol before the gaoler fell desperately in love with her, and they fled together. At a short distance from Cattanzaro they were met by her brothers, also brigands. They immediately slew the gaoler, who was of no further use, and Maria formed a new band of brigands, of which she was made captain, and commenced ravaging the tract of mountainous country lying between Cattanzaro and the river Crati. The reckless, useless acts of cruelty excited the indignation of the people for miles round. She sacked the villages of Spinelli, Cotzenei, and Belvedere; and in spite of the exertions made by the Italian Government of the province, who, in the autumn of 1864, despatched two battalions of the line in pursuit of the band, the rural population were in such dread of Maria that the soldiers could do nothing.

Another locally famous brigand, Crouo Donatello, was accompanied in his campaigns by his *inamorata*, who was as brave as he. In an encounter with the royal troops in August or September, 1863, Donatello, compelled to fly, left behind him this woman, who fought desperately before letting herself be taken.

In 1866, in a skirmish between the Papal troops and the brigands in the neighbourhood of the Eternal City, two of the latter were slain. One of the corpses proved to be that of a large, good-looking peasant woman, about thirty years of age, armed and dressed like her comrades. She was subsequently recognised as the wife of the bandit chief Cedrone; and the latter was inconsolable for the loss of his brave spouse, being seen for days and days to weep bitterly, though his followers surrounded him, proffering empty consolations.

The famous Brigand Pietro Bianchi, some eighteen or nineteen years since the terror of the district of Nicastro, in the Calabrian mountains, was accompanied in nearly every expedition by a girl named Generosa Cardamone (aged about seventeen in 1861, the chief himself being then twenty), who might frequently be seen on horseback at the head of the band, encouraging them in the fight. In point of ferocity and ruthless courage she was worthy of her lover—nay, she far surpassed him, and is said to have repeatedly cooked human flesh, and served it up to him and his followers. Bianchi loved the young and beautiful demon most passionately, and was madly jealous of her. One day a bandit kissed her, but his audacity was instantly punished by a score of dagger-stabs dealt by the unerring hand of his chief. Generosa was deeply religious after a fashion, and marvellously superstitious; when she was arrested, in 1867, a religious book and a Madonna were found upon her, which she carried, through a blind idea that they rendered her invulnerable.

In March, 1867, a lieutenant of gendarmes discovered the cave of Bianchi at Soveria, and with his own men, aided by a detachment of the line, forced the brigand and his mistress to surrender, after they had been the terror of the country for seven years.

De Martino, for some time the worst and most ferocious bandit in the Abruzzi, was likewise accompanied by his paramour, who had the character of being more cruel than he was himself. For months the Royal troops were engaged constantly hunting them up and down the woods. At last, in August, 1869, they discovered and surrounded the lurking place of De Martino. The brigand, firing upon the carabineers, by mishap set the dry twigs of the hut in a blaze, and was burnt alive, together with the partner of his crimes.

Duke Ernest of Saxe-Coburg Gotha, on the occasion of the 25th anniversary of his accession, February, 1869, founded an Order of Decoration to recompense courage in women.

The Franco-Prussian War, and the subsequent Communist Insurrection, proved that the military spirit was not extinct in the hearts of women, and that modern female warriors were as ready and as eager for the fray as any of their ancestresses. But the numerous newspaper anecdotes and reports were in many instances more or less creations of fancy, often false, frequently written in haste, as a rule full of gross exaggerations, whether emanating from French or German quarters, consequently always unreliable. One of the most remarkable and best authenticated female warriors of the period was Minna Hänsel, of Berlin, who, in the early days of the war, before the Germans had swept all before them, raised an Amazon corps, all ready equipped and full of military ardour. These warlike women were much ridiculed by the Berlinese, but the Fräulein Hänsel, disregarding the adverse criticism which, she said, was "of course only to be expected in these frivolous days of ours," addressed a letter to the Governor of the city, General Von Falkenstein, asking him in what place the services of the corps would prove most effective. The General—purposely, perhaps—delayed returning an answer till the closing days of August, 1870, when Miss Hänsel, although her offers of service had by no means been rejected, considered that the "rapid and victorious progress of the war" put an end to any necessity for her corps being employed, and accordingly disbanded her troop.

A wounded soldier in November, 1870, passed through Berlin, and was the object of general attention. This soldier was a young woman only twenty-four, carefully educated, but imbued with a strong bias in favour of masculine dress and an active life. She passed the ensign's examinations, and, with good recommendations, entered the army under the name of Weiss. She distinguished herself by the recovery of a Prussian standard, which had been taken by the enemy, and was presented with the Iron Cross. Having received four shot wounds, she was sent for recovery to her native place, Tilsit.

But the hurried, fragmentary mention of either French or German "heroines" is hardly worth serious record or investigation. To ascertain the truth or the falsity of any one anecdote would be now clearly impossible. That noble spirit and patriotic ardour glowed on both sides throughout the desperate struggle is without a doubt; and in the universal enthusiasm women shared as freely as their fellow-countrymen, and were ready to spend life and treasure in the service of their native land and national honour.

IV.

INDIA.—Indian Amazons—Cleophes, Queen of Massaga—Moynawoti, Queen of Kamrup—Ranee of Scinde—Sultana Rizia—Gool Behisht—Booboojee Khanum and Dilshad Agha, Mother and Aunt of a King of Bijapur—Durgautti, Queen of Gurrah—Khunza Sultana, Regent of Ahmednuggur—Chand Sultana, Regent of Ahmednuggur—Nour Mahal, Empress of Hindostan — Princess Janee Begum — Juliana — Madam Mequinez, Colonel in the Service of Hyder Ali Khan—Begum Somroo, General in the Service of the Emperor Shah Aulum—Begum Nujuf Cooli—Mrs. W., Wife of a British Sergeant—Lukshmi Baee, Ranee of Jhansi—Female Mutineer captured before Delhi, 1857—Female Guards in the Zenanas of Indian Princes—Begum of Oude—Female Soldiers in Bantam.

THE early history of India is involved in such deep obscurity that we have no reliable information before the invasion of Alexander the great. True, we read of a nation of Indian Amazons, mentioned by Nonnus, but we have no details on the subject. Amongst the sovereigns who opposed the invincible Macedonian, was Cleophes, Queen of Massaga, whose capital city was said to have been impregnable. While reconnoitring the fortress, Alexander was wounded in the leg. But without waiting for the wound to heal, he commenced battering the walls with various military engines of the most redoubtable aspect; which so terrified the Queen, who had never even heard of anything like them, that she speedily tendered her submission. Alexander, who merely conquered cities for the sake of glory, permitted her to retain all her dominions in peace.

In Martin's " History of Eastern India " we read of a warrior-queen named Moynawoti. She was married to Manikechandro, brother of Dhormo Pal, a King of Kamrup, and on the death of her husband, she made war on the king, who was defeated and slain on the banks of the Tista. Gopichondro, son of Moynawoti, succeeded his uncle on the throne, but he left the management of state affairs to his mother, and gave himself up to a life of pleasure. When he grew up, however, the young king wished to take an active share in the government, but his mother persuaded him to dedicate his life to religion, and he ever after practised the utmost humility and self-denial.

It was during the caliphate of Walid that the Mahommedans made their first conquests beyond the Indus. About the year 711 A.D., an Arab ship having been seized at Dival, or Dewal, a port connected with Scinde, Hejaj, the Moslem governor of Bosra, demanded its restitution. Daher, Rajah of Scinde, refused; and this led to the invasion of India by six thousand followers of Islam. Daher marched at the head of fifty thousand men to oppose the invaders, but in the battle which ensued he was slain, and his troops routed with terrible slaughter.

Daher's widow, with a courage worthy her deceased lord, raised fifteen thousand men, and offered battle to the conquerors. They declined the challenge, and she retired within the walls of Adjur. The Moslems closely invested the city; and the garrison, reduced to the last extremities, sacrificed their wives and children on the burning pile formed by their gold and treasures, and, headed by the royal widow, attacked the besiegers in their own camp. They all fell, fighting gallantly to the last.

On the death of Altumsh, Emperor of Hindostan, in 1235, he was succeeded by his son, Prince Feroze. The latter was an effeminate, luxurious monarch, who thought of nothing but spending on dancing-women, comedians, and musicians, the treasures accumulated by his father, and he left the affairs of state to be ruled by his mother. Her cruelty, and the indifference of Feroze, caused several of the omrahs to revolt. The emperor marched against them with a vast army; but he was deserted by his vizier, a great portion of his army, and seven of his principal nobles. The latter returned to Delhi, and placed Sultana Rizia, the eldest daughter of Altumsh, on the throne. When this news reached Feroze, he hastened back to Delhi; but the new Empress marched out to meet him, and he was delivered into her hands. He died in confinement some time after.

The Sultana possessed every quality proper for a ruler; even detractors could find no fault, save that she was a woman. During her father's lifetime she had entered heartily into state affairs and was Regent for a short time during the absence of Altumsh on an expedition against Gwalior.

Rizia was not long left in undisturbed possession of the throne. The omrahs who had conspired against her brother now marched from Lahore, and encamped before Delhi; but she contrived to sow dissensions amongst them, and each was compelled to retreat to his own province. Some of them, pursued by the Empress, were captured and put to death. The omrahs finally tendered their submission and the empire enjoyed peace for a time. But the promotion of Jammal, who had once been an Abyssinian slave, to the post of Captain-general of Hindostan, gave such umbrage to the nobles as to ruin the cause of Rizia. The viceroy of Lahore threw off his allegiance in 1239; but the empress, collecting her forces, marched against him, and the viceroy was compelled to accept peace on the most humiliating terms.

Scarcely was this revolt quelled, when Altunia, governor of Tiberhind, raised the standard of rebellion. Rizia immediately marched against him; but when she had gone about halfway, all the Turkish chiefs mutinied. A tumultuous scene ensued, the Abyssinian general was slain, and the Empress sent prisoner to Tiberhind. The imperial troops then returned to Delhi; and set Byram, the Empress's younger brother, upon the throne.

Rizia married the Governor of Tiberhind, and by their joint influence they raised a great army, and marched to Delhi. They were defeated near the city, by the troops of Byram, and the empress with difficulty escaped to Tiberhind. Soon, however, she rallied her scattered forces, and marched once more towards the capital. But she was again defeated at Keitel, and, together with her husband, made prisoner, and barbarously put to death. Thus died Sultana Rizia, after a brief reign of three years six months and six days. Indian historians agree that she was worthy of of a better fate.

One day the Emperor Alla-a-Deen Khiljy was

boasting that no rajah throughout Hindostan would dare to oppose his power. Nehr Dew, Rajah of Jalwur, "in the plenitude of his folly," exclaimed, "I will suffer death if I do not raise an army that shall defeat any attempt of the king's troop to take the fort of Jalwur."

The Emperor, in a rage, commanded the rajah to quit Delhi. Hearing, shortly after, that Nehr Dew was raising forces, he ordered a division of his army to besiege Jalwur. This was in 1309. To signalize his contempt for the rajah, he placed the troops under the command of a slave girl of the palace, named Gool Behisht, or, "the Rose of Heaven." She displayed great courage during the siege, and had almost effected the capture of Jalwur, when she was seized with a mortal illness. On her death the command was given to her son, Shaheen. Nehr Dew made a sortie, defeated the imperial forces, and slew Shaheen with his own hand. The Emperor, enraged at this defeat, sent reinforcements to renew the siege; Jalwur was taken, and Nehr Dew, with his family, and the whole of the garrison, put to the sword.

In 1510 Ismail Adil Shah ascended the throne of Bijapur. Being too young to rule the state, the administration was entrusted to Kumal Khan Deccany, the most powerful noble in the land. The latter soon made up his mind to usurp the throne;

and in the following year he found himself in a position to make the attempt.

He was warned by the astrologers that certain days in the present month were unfavourable to his designs; and recommended to avoid approaching any one of whom he had suspicions. The regent, acting on their advice, committed the charge of the citadel to his own adherents, and shut himself up with his family in a house close by the royal palace.

Booboojee Khanum, the queen-mother, now resolved by a bold stroke to get rid of the regent. Affecting uneasiness about his health, she despatched one of her adherents with secret instructions for the assassination of Kumal Khan. The plot succeeded, though the murderer was immediately cut to pieces. The regent's mother, with great presence of mind, commanded the attendants to keep silent, and sent orders to Sufdur Khan, the son of Kumal Khan, to seize the king at once. Sufdur closed the gates of the citadel and advanced with a strong force to the palace. The queen-mother would have submitted, but for Dilshad Agha, the king's foster-aunt, who declared that in such a crisis valour was better than submission. She ordered the palace gates to be closed, and sent out to the Persians, on duty in the outer court of the seraglio, entreating them to assist their king against his enemies. The foreign generals declared their readiness to defend the young prince.

Dilshad Agha and the queen-mother came out on the battlements, clad in armour, with bows and arrows in their hands. They were accompanied by Ismail Adil Shah, who had the yellow umbrella of his father held over his head by a Turkish girl named Murtufa.

Sufdur Khan tried to force open the gates, but was met with volleys of arrows; the king, his mother and aunt, and Murtufa using the bow with considerable effect. The brave little band were reinforced presently by fifty Deccany matchlock-men; and several score of foreigners from the city; but though the besiegers were thus kept in check, their force was so considerably superior in numbers that they continued the assault with the utmost fury, fully confident of ultimate victory.

Dilshad Agha, with a veil thrown over her face, fought with bow and arrow in the ranks of the soldiers, encouraging them by exciting speeches and promises. Sufdur Khan at last made a desperate attack with five hundred men, bringing cannon to batter the walls; and the royal adherents fell in great numbers. Some fled ignominiously, while the rest, concealing themselves behind the parapet, remained perfectly still. The enemy, believing that all the garrison had taken to flight, burst open the outer gate; but while he was endeavouring to force the inner door, Dilshad Agha gave orders for her troops to discharge a volley of shot and arrows, which committed fearful havoc in the enemy's ranks, and pierced the eye of Sufdur Khan. The latter ran under the terrace on which the royalists stood; and the king, rolling down a heavy stone, crushed his enemy to death.

The death of Sufdur put an end to the rebellion. The insurgents, giving themselves up for lost, opened the gates of the citadel, and fled. By the advice of Dilshad Agha, the heads of the regent and his son were displayed through the streets of the city.

During the reign of Akbar the Great, Emperor of Hindostan, that part of the Deccan which now comprises Orissa and Bundelcund, was known by the name of Gurrah, and was governed by a warlike queen, named Durgautti, equally distinguished for her beauty, her accomplishments, and the talented manner in which she conducted the affairs of her kingdom. She succeeded to the throne on the death of her husband. The country was about one hundred and fifty crores in length and about fifty in breadth; yet so prosperous, that it contained upwards of seventy thousand towns and villages, closely populated.

About the year 1564, Asaf Khan Hirvys, an Indian noble, was raised by the emperor to the rank of an Omrah of five thousand, and appointed governor of

Kurrah and Mannichpoor. The new Omrah at once began a series of predatory incursions into Gurrah; and very soon he invaded the country with an army of about twelve thousand foot and five or six hundred horse. Durgautti assembled eight thousand horse, fifteen hundred elephants, and a few hundred foot, and advanced to meet the invaders. Clad in armour, a helmet on her head, a lance grasped in her right hand, a bow and a quiver lying by her side, she led her troops to battle, riding in a howdah on the back of an elephant. Though the men were totally unaccustomed to war, the love of liberty and the example of the Queen raised their courage to such a pitch that, in their eagerness to fight, they marched too rapidly, and would speedily have become an undisciplined mob. But Durgautti, perceiving the cause of their disorder, commanded a halt; and after re-forming their broken ranks, she gave them strict orders to march slowly, as compactly as they could, and not to engage the foe until they saw the signal displayed from the elephant of the royal standard.

A sanguinary battle then ensued, in which Durgautti displayed the greatest courage. After a long and obstinate conflict, the Mahommedans were routed, with a loss of eight hundred slain. The queen pursued the flying enemy till night put an end to the contest. She then halted, and gave orders for the soldiers to wash and refresh themselves, preparatory to a night attack on the camp of Asaf Khan; but her vizier and the remainder of her generals refused to aid in a night assault, and seditiously demanded permission to inter their fallen comrades. She unwillingly consented; and when the bodies of the slain had been burned, she entreated the chiefs, one by one, to assist her in an assault on the Mogul camp. But all in vain. Not one would second her in this daring enterprise.

Asaf Khan, seeing what kind of enemy he had to do with, advanced next morning with the heavy guns, which, on account of the bad state of the roads, he had not been able to use in the previous action. Durgautti posted her men at a narrow pass, and prepared to meet the enemy once more. Asaf, with his cannon, soon opened a lane into the open ground beyond, where the forces of Gurrah were drawn up. The Rajah Beir Shaw, Durgautti's son, a young man of great promise, displayed great bravery in a charge. Twice he repulsed the Moguls; in the third attack he was severely wounded. He was falling from his horse when the queen, who was in the front of the battle, mounted on her elephant, perceived that her son was expiring, and called to some of her attendants to carry him to the rear. Several crowded round him, glad of some excuse to quit the field. The death of this young man and the retreat of so many of her soldiers struck terror into the queen's army. Durgautti was soon left with only three hundred men on the field; yet she held her ground, determined to conquer or die. At last her eye was pierced by an arrow. She tried to extricate it, but it broke off near the end, leaving a piece of the steel barb sticking in the wound. At this moment another arrow pierced her neck. This she pulled out; but a mist swam before her eyes, and for a few moments she was seen to rock to and fro in her howdah.

Adhar, a brave officer of her household, who drove her elephant, repulsed numbers of the enemy. Perceiving that the day was irretrievably lost, he entreated the queen to let him take her from the field, but Durgautti would not hear of it. She begged of him to stab her to the heart. He refused, and Durgautti, suddenly leaning forward, snatched a dagger from his belt, plunged it into her heart, and immediately expired.

With her death the triumph of Asaf Khan was complete. The queen's youngest son, a mere infant, was trodden to death soon after, at the capture of Chouraghus, and the whole country submitted to the Moguls.

About this time, another warlike queen, Khunza Sultana, was Regent of Ahmednuggur. During the minority of her son, Murtuza Nizam Shah, she transacted the affairs of the state, while he was engaged in amusements suitable to his age. In 1566, Ally Adil Shah, King of Bijapur, having invaded the neighbouring state of Bijanuggur, Venkatradry, the Hindoo chief of that country, applied for assistance to Khunza Sultana. She marched at the head of a large force against Bijapur, and obliged the king to return and defend his own dominions. However, peace was soon re-established between the two Mohammedan states, and a league formed against the Peishwah of Berar. The united forces of Ahmednuggur and Bijapur entered that country, plundered it, and marched home again, laden with booty. On the homeward march, Ally Adil Shah treacherously endeavoured to seize the young King of Ahmednuggur. But Khunza Sultana, learning his designs, decamped during the night, and a river, which intervened, having swelled, the two armies were effectually separated before morning.

The sultana, however, gave great umbrage to the nobles by providing for her own relations at the expense of more deserving men. In 1567, several rajahs formed a conspiracy against her, and induced the young king to join them. But the latter, afraid of his mother's ire, betrayed the plot to her, and the ringleaders were all seized.

In 1569, the dowager queen, with her son, marched

against Kishwur Khan, the Bijapur general, who had invaded the state of Ahmednuggur. When they reached D'hamungam, Murtuza Nizam Shah resolved to free himself from his mother's trammels, gained over the principal nobles, and sent one of them to inform her that it was his royal will she should no longer meddle in public affairs. Furious at this unlooked-for audacity, Khunza assembled her attendants, threw a veil over her face, and rode out of the palace on horseback, armed with a sword and dagger. She was seized after a short struggle, and her people took to flight. Thenceforth, Khunza Sultana lived in retirement, never again interfering in public matters.

In 1594 died Burhan Nizam Shah, King of Ahmednuggur. His son, Ibrahim Nizam Shah, who succeeded him, was slain in battle, and the vizier, Meean Munjoo, raised to the throne a boy named Ahmed, said to belong to the royal family. The nobles refused to acknowledge the new king, and besieged the vizier in the capital. Unable to contend with them, the vizier solicited aid from the Moguls, promising to put the fort of Ahmednuggur into their hands.

The Moguls had long sought an excuse to interfere in the affairs of Ahmednuggur; so Murad Mirza, son of the Emperor Akbar, marched thither with great expedition, being joined on his road by several rajahs and generals with their troops. But Meean Munjoo, having suppressed the rebellion, in place of surrendering the fort, resolved to defend it in case he was called upon by the Moguls to fulfil his promise. After laying in a store of provisions, he gave the command to the Princess Chand Beeby, daughter of a former King of Ahmednuggur, and departed with the young Prince Ahmed towards the Bijapur frontier.

Chand Beeby was one of the ablest Indian politicians of her time. She had been for some years queen and dowager-regent of Bijapur. She now took the entire direction of affairs into her own hands; in a few days she had raised her own nephew, Bahadur Nizam Shah, to the throne, though he was at this time a prisoner in a distant fortress, and seemed likely to stay there.

The Moguls, seeing that it was useless to conceal their hostile intentions, prepared openly to besiege Ahmednuggur. On the 14th December, 1595, the first shots were exchanged. The siege was pressed with the utmost vigour. Mounds were raised, trenches opened, battery after battery erected, mines sunk; and on the morning of February 17th, 1596, eighty feet of wall were blown down by the explosion of a mine. Chand Beeby, though many of her principal officers had taken to flight, was not dismayed. She put on armour, covered her face with a veil, and, grasping a drawn sword in her hand, rushed to defend the breach. This intrepidity shamed the fugitives, and re-animated the panic-stricken soldiers. Recovering from their first terror, the soldiers calmly awaited the approach of the Mogul storming-party. An obstinate conflict ensued at the foot of the breach. Again and again did the Moguls press onward—again and again they were driven back by a galling fire of shot and rockets. The ditch was soon more than half filled with dead and dying warriors. Although fresh storming parties succeeded one another from four o'clock in the afternoon till dark, they were all repulsed with fearful slaughter. At last the Moguls withdrew, discomfited, to their camp.

Deccan traditions say that, during the storm, the shot of the garrison having become exhausted, Chand Beeby ordered the guns to be loaded, first with copper coins, then with silver, and at length with gold; and all the coins being likewise used up, she fired away her jewels.

The valour of Chand Beeby formed the chief subject of conversation round the camp-fires and in the tents of the Moguls; and, after this memorable day, her title of Chand Beeby, "the Lady Chand," was changed by common consent to the grander one of Chand Sultana.

The want of provisions, and the approach of seventy thousand men from Bijapur, compelled the Moguls to retreat a few days after the storm. Bahadur Shah was now brought from the fort of Chawund, where he had been held prisoner, and was placed on the throne. But the ambition and duplicity of the Ahmednuggur nobles brought about a second siege in 1599. Chand Sultana, afraid to trust any of them, applied to Humeed Khan, an officer of high rank, who recommended her to defend the place to the last extremity; but Chand declared that so many chiefs had acted treacherously, it was plain no reliance could be placed on them, and she proposed that they should negotiate with the besiegers. Humeed Khan rushed into the streets, crying out that Chand Sultana was treating with the Moguls to surrender the fort. The ungrateful and short-sighted mob, believing him, and forgetting the former services of the heroine, rushed to the private apartments of Chand Sultana, and murdered her in their fury.

It is satisfactory to know that the ungrateful people got the reward they so richly merited. For, a few days after the death of Chand, the Moguls captured the fort, giving little or no quarter.

Mher-Ul-Nissa, or Nour Mahal, the " Light of the Harem," sometimes styled Nour Jehan, the " Light of the World," was the favourite Sultana of Jehanghire, the "World-subduing Emperor" of Hindostan. A romantic story is told of her strange birth, her desertion by her parents, and how, like Moses, she was entrusted to the care of her own mother by her kind preserver, and how, by the benevolence of the latter, the family rose from poverty and obscurity to the government of the greatest empire in Asia. The beauty of Nour Mahal was famous throughout the East; Moore, in his "Feast of Roses," has painted her portrait most exquisitely. Her personal charms were rivalled by her mental powers; and her political talents were speedily seen by the numerous reforms and improvements effected throughout the empire.

Nour Mahal was a widow when, in 1611, she became the bride of Jehanghire, and it is said that she took for her second husband the murderer of her first. Her influence over the Emperor soon became paramount. They had many tastes in common, amongst others the passion for hunting; Nour Mahal was as fond of the chase as Zenobia. In company with Jehanghire she would slay tigers and other savage beasts of the jungle, charming her lord by the adroitness with which she handled the bow or the more unwieldy matchlock.

It was strange that a haughty, overbearing, courageous woman like Nour Mahal should never have taken command of an army. We read of only one battle in which she was personally engaged. Her policy was to choose able generals to conduct all her wars. However, one of these chieftains was near causing her ruin. This was Mohabat Khan, the most talented Indian warrior of his time. She had the folly to quarrel with this man, and he, seeing that his ruin was determined upon, took the initiative, and seized the emperor in his own camp. He soon saw that it would have been wiser to arrest the empress; but on returning to remedy this fault, he found she had fled to the camp of her brother, on the other bank of the river—the Chenab.

Next morning the empress led a party across the river to rescue Jehanghire. She was armed with a bow and two quivers of arrows, and sat in a howdah on the back of an elephant. In fording the stream, hundreds were swept away by the force of the current. Those who escaped drowning were weighed down by their armour and their wet clothes, and had their powder spoilt. In this disastrous condition they were obliged to fight hand to hand with the rebels before a landing could be effected. Nour Mahal, with her brother and a handful of the bravest chiefs, was amongst the first who reached the shore; but this little band could make no impression on the ranks of Mohabat Khan, whose soldiers poured volley after volley, shot, arrows, and rockets, upon the men struggling in the water. The ford was soon choked up with men, horses, and elephants, dead or dying.

The contest raged fiercest round the elephant of Nour Mahal, who never quailed before the infuriated rebels who sought her life. Her gallant defenders fell one after another, fighting manfully to the last; but she herself appeared to bear a charmed life amidst the perfect hail of bullets and winged shafts, though her infant granddaughter, who sat close beside her, was wounded, the driver of her elephant was shot, and the beast himself received a cut across the trunk. Half-maddened with pain, the animal plunged into the river, and was carried away by the stream. When at length the elephant struggled up the bank, Nour Mahal was discovered calmly extracting an arrow from the wound of her grandchild, as cool and collected as though she had been a spectator at a review in place of the leading actor in a fierce encounter. The howdah was saturated with blood.

The failure of this rash, though gallant attempt, proved that Mohabat was too strong to be subdued by open force; Nour Mahal therefore resolved to lull his suspicions, and trust to chance for some expedient to crush him. Next day she went to his camp and surrendered herself a prisoner. For a time Mohabat Khan ruled paramount throughout the empire; but in a few months Nour Mahal, partly by cunning, partly by appealing to the loyalty of the omrahs, rescued her husband from the clutches of this man, whose power thenceforth ceased for ever.

Jehanghire died on the 28th of October, 1627.

Although Nour Mahal survived him for twenty-four years, she held aloof from politics. She was buried in a splendid tomb at Lahore, close by the monument of Jehanghire.

Spontini has chosen the story of Nour Mahal as the subject for one of his best operas.

In 1688 the Mogul army, commanded by Azim Shah (son of Aurengzebe) was engaged in the siege of Bijapur. The troops were much distressed for want of provisions, as their supplies had been cut off by the enemy. Aurengzebe, hearing of this, ordered one of his generals to take twenty thousand bullock-loads of grain to the camp of Azim Shah. The enemy made a desperate attempt to seize this convoy on its road; but after a fierce encounter with the Moguls, they were driven off. During the action, the Princess Janee Begum, who was proceeding with the convoy to join her husband, Azim Shah, rode on the back of an elephant into the midst of the fight, and encouraged the soldiers by her presence.

Juliana is perhaps the only European woman who ever took a leading part in the politics of the court of Delhi. She was born in Bengal in 1658, and her father was a Portuguese gentleman, named Augustin Dias D'Acosta. Early in life she gained the favour of Aurengzebe, who made her superintendent of his Zenana, and governess of his son, Bahadur Shah.

In 1707 Aurengzebe died, and Bahadur Shah ascended the throne. His right was disputed by his brothers, and he was compelled to defend his throne by force of arms. A battle was fought near Agra; Juliana, mounted on an elephant, by the side of Bahadur Shah, aided him by her advice, and cheered him with inspiring words; when his troops began to give way, she exhorted him not to despair. To her presence indeed was he indebted for the ultimate victory gained by his army.

Juliana was created a princess, and given the rank of wife of an omrah, together with innumerable honours and riches showered upon her. The Great Mogul held her in such estimation that he used to say:—"If Juliana were a man, I would make her my vizier."

Jehandur Shah, who ascended the throne in 1712, entertained the same respect for Juliana. She experienced some persecutions when this emperor was deposed in 1713 by his nephew Ferokshere; but the death of this tyrant, in 1719, restored to her all her influence, which she retained till her death, in 1733.

During the latter half of the eighteenth century, the native princes of India finding, by dearly bought experience, that Indian discipline was ludicrously inferior to the European system, determined to introduce the latter into their own battalions. With this view they offered high rewards to European officers who would accept the command of their troops and teach them how to fight. Hundreds of adventurers—British, French, German, Swiss, Portuguese—soldiers of fortune, in short, from every part of Europe, took service under the various rajahs and princes, and many of them attained to high rank and honours. It was not uncommon for the widows of these officers to be given the post left vacant by their deceased husbands; and these female commanders led their troops to battle, or stopped at home, as they pleased.

One of these soldiers of fortune was Colonel Mequinez, a Portuguese, who commanded a regiment of Topasses in the service of Hyder Ali Khan, Sultan of Mysore. At his death, Hyder Ali gave the widow (also a Portuguese) the command of her husband's regiment, to hold it till the adopted son of her husband had attained his majority. Madam

Mequinez never went into action; she left the duty of leading the Topasses in the field to the officer next in command. But in every other respect she fulfilled the duties of colonel; the colours were carried to her house, at the door of which a sentry paced up and down: she received the pay for the entire corps, and caused the deductions for each company to be made in her presence, and she always inspected the regiment herself.

Madam Mequinez was excessively avaricious, besides having a character for immorality. Having been detected in a plot to cheat the Provincial Father of the Mysore Jesuits out of a large sum in rupees and jewels, she was excommunicated, and sentenced to undergo public penance. Some months latter she finally disgraced herself by marrying a "mongrel Portuguese sergeant" belonging to her regiment. But she was very much surprised when the bacsi informed her that the Sultan had reduced her pay to that of a sergeant, because she had brought shame on the memory of her first husband, who had been a great favourite with the Sultan, Hyder Ali.

One of the most thoroughly unprincipled European adventurers of these days was Somroo, a German soldier, who, after serving as private in the French and English armies, and in those of various native chiefs, became general in the army of the Great Mogul. His name was Gualtier Reignard, or Reinehard, but when he enlisted in the French army (in Europe) he assumed the *nom de guerre* of Summer, which his comrades, on account of his saturnine complexion, altered to Sombre; this, the Hindoos changed to Somroo, and he was afterwards best known by this last name. He will ever remain infamous as the murderer of two hundred English prisoners at Patna, in 1763. While in the service of Shah Aulum, the Emperor, he commanded a body of cavalry and several disciplined battalions of sepoys officered by Europeans. To maintain this army, the emperor assigned him, as a jaghire, the fertile district of Serdhauna, in the Dooab.

Somroo married twice; his second wife was, some say, the daughter of a Mogul noble who had fallen into great distress, though others aver she was a Cashmerian dancing-girl. He persuaded the Begum to renounce Mohammedanism and become a Roman Catholic. At Somroo's death, in 1778, the Vizier Nujeef Khan gave the widow the jaghire and the military post. She was a great favourite with the Emperor, who had the highest respect for her talents. He bestowed upon her the name of Zul Al Nissa, which means "Ornament of her sex." Under the government of this talented woman the "small but fertile" town of Serdhauna improved rapidly. A fort standing a short distance from the town served as a kind of citadel, and contained a barrack, an arsenal, and a foundry for cannon. Her five battalions of sepoys were officered from nearly every country in Europe, and she had a body of five hundred European artillerymen, armed with forty guns of various calibre.

George Thomas, afterwards the most famous of all these European soldiers of fortune, accepted a commission in the Begum's service; and her keen eyes quickly discerned his superior military talent. He soon rose to high favour with the Begum, whose esteem he merited by courage, zeal, and untiring activity. So greatly was her revenue and authority increased by his talents, that he was for many years her chief counsellor and adviser.

Begum Somroo enjoyed the respect of the leading ministers at the court of Delhi; the Viziers Nujeef Khan, Mirza Shuffee, and Afrasiab Khan placed the most implicit trust in her judgment on military matters. When Scindiah, the Mahratta chief, attained to the rank of vizier, he not only confirmed her in the jaghire of Serdhauna, but added a grant of territory south-west of the Jumna. Her generalship was not confined to occasional reviews; she took an active part in the wars and insurrections which disturbed the reign of Shah Aulem. During the war with Pertaub Sing, the

Begum was stationed with her troops at Panniput; which being an important post, proves Scindiah's belief in her military capacities.

In 1787, during the insurrection of Gholaum Cadir Khan, Prince of Sehraurunpore, Begum Somroo displayed the utmost coolness and determination. Previous to his open declaration of hostility, Gholaum, by the most artful speeches, endeavoured to gain the Begum's alliance; well aware of her influence at court, he offered her an equal share in the administration if she would assist him in seizing the reins of government. The proposal was tempting, but the Begum, well acquainted with the perfidious nature of the wily Rohilla chief, rejected all his offers, and repaired to the palace, where she announced her resolve to sacrifice life itself, if necessary, in defence of her sovereign.

Her arrival infused new courage into the Imperial party; and some of the generals having assembled their forces, Gholaum Cadir opened a heavy cannonade on the palace. This was answered from the fort of Delhi; and after the bombardment had lasted for several hours, the rebel chief receiving intelligence that a large force was marching to relieve the Emperor, judged it most prudent to tender an apology, which Shah Aulem thought fit to accept.

In the following year, 1788, Shah Aulem left

Delhi with a large army, partly made up by three battalions of sepoys, commanded by the Begum, and commenced a tour through the provinces. Although most of the rajahs and nabobs were secretly disaffected, they were, with few exceptions, easily prevailed upon to tender their submission. One of those who openly declared themselves rebels was Nujuff Cooli Khan, a powerful chief, who, having possession of the almost impregnable fort of Gocul Ghur, peremptorily refused to submit. His head-quarters were situated at a village about a mile from the fort, and only a portion of his army had been stationed in Gocul Ghur.

The Emperor himself, with the main body of the army, invested Gocul Ghur, while two of his principal generals erected batteries against the rebel head-quarters, which they bombarded most vigorously. The village would have speedily been taken, but for the disgraceful conduct of the besieging force, both officers and men, who gave themselves up to riot and excess. Nujuff Cooli Khan, taking advantage of this, atacked the Mogul entrenchments one night, when nearly all the soldiers were fast asleep. Carrying all before them, the rebels perpetrated an indiscriminate slaughter before the others had time to arouse themselves. This news rapidly spread to the main body and threw the whole camp into dire confusion. To increase the consternation, Munsoor Khan sallied out from Gocul Ghur, and opened a tremendous cannonade on the rear of the camp.

The entire Imperial army, together with Shah Aulem and his family, would probably have fallen into the hands of the rebels, but for the courage and presence of mind of Begum Somroo. She was encamped with her sepoys to the right of the camp, and her troops not having been infected by the panic, waited, drawn up ready for action. Perceiving the disorder which prevailed, the Begum sent a respectful message to Shah Aulem, entreating him to repair for safety to her quarters. Then, stepping into her palanquin, she proceeded at the head of one hundred sepoys and a six-pounder (the latter commanded by a European) to the ground occupied by Munsoor Khan. She ordered her palanquin to be set down, and ere long drove the rebels from the field by a well-directed fire of grape, supported by volleys of musketry from the sepoys.

This gallant exploit gave time for the Imperial troops to rally. In their turn they now attacked the rebels, and after a short sharply contested engagement, the latter were defeated. Nujuff Cooli Khan, disheartened by this reverse, entreated the Begum to intercede for his pardon; which was granted at last, after he had paid a large sum of money into the Imperial treasury.

In 1791, Nujuff Cooli Khan again broke into rebellion. Ismail Beg was despatched to arrest him; but when the latter reached Rewari, where the rebel chief had set up his head-quarters, he learned that Nujuff was dead. However, the widow of Nujuff Cooli, a woman akin to Begum Somroo, of a masculine spirit, possessing, moreover, considerable military abilities, took command of deceased's forces. Knowing that Ismaeel Beg was courageous, talented, and ambitious, she proposed an alliance, which he accepted; and throwing himself into the town of Canoor, defended it against the Mahrattas. The Begum displayed the utmost courage throughout the siege, and invariably joined in all the sorties made by the garrison. Unfortunately, this brave woman was slain in a skirmish by a cannon-ball, and her death broke up the rebel camp. It was resolved by the garrison to deliver up Ismaeel Beg to the Mahrattas; but he was beforehand with them, and surrendered the town.

General Thomas, in his zeal for the Begum Somroo's interests, raised up enemies for himself in the principal French and German officers. They took occasion to poison the Begum's mind against him by foul accusations; and in 1792 he was compelled to withdraw to Anopsheer, one of the frontier stations of the British army. Early in 1793, he took service under Appakandarow, a Mahratta chieftain. Le

Vaissaux, or Levasso, a German adventurer, commanding the Begum's artillery, had always been Thomas's deadly foe, and was the leading man in driving him away. He possessed great military talents, and had rendered considerable services to his mistress; but he was a man of haughty, overbearing mien, and hated by all his brother-officers. Great was their indignation, though they were scarcely surprised, when the Begum, disregarding their remonstrances, and the advice, the all but commands, of the Emperor, surrendered her hand and heart to the German artilleryman, in 1793.

Begum Somroo, instigated by her husband, now determined to crush poor Thomas; and at the head of four battalions of foot, four hundred horse, and twenty pieces of cannon, she marched towards Jyjur, where he was stationed. But the Mahratta chiefs, who had long been jealous of her influence over Shah Aulem, stirred up a mutiny amongst the troops left in Serdhauna, and compelled her to return thither with all speed. The officers, to give a sanction to their proceedings, offered the jaghire to Zuffer Yab Khan, son of Somroo by a former wife. He was a young man of worthless and turbulent character; since his father's death he had lived in Delhi, receiving a handsome allowance from his stepmother.

It was only a few days after the marriage that this

mutiny broke out. Zuffer, with a body of troops, rushed into Serdhauna, seized the town, and was proclaimed Jaghire Dar. The Begum vainly endeavoured to pacify her soldiers, She was arrested, together with her husband, and thrown into prison; and Le Vaissaux, too proud to sue for mercy, put an end to his own life.

In the course of the following year, the Begum, who had been ever since kept in durance vile, besought the assistance of George Thomas, for, said she, the hourly dread of assassination was driving her mad. Thomas was not deaf to her entreaties; he persuaded Bappoo, a Mahratta chief, to aid him with his forces, and together they marched upon Serdhauna. The Mahrattas were won over, partly by the prayers of Shah Aulem, and partly by liberal promises; and Zuffer having been expelled, the Begum was restored to power.

Begum Sumroo was a good friend to the English, with whom she was always exceedingly popular on account of the great hospitality with which she entertianed those who visited her neighbourhood. However, she fought against them, as an auxiliary of Scindiah, in 1803. She took part in the battle of Assaye; and at the defeat of the Mahrattas, she fled to Northern Hindostan, and hastily made peace with the Marquis Wellesley, on condition that her principality should revert to the British Government of

India after her demise, while her personal property remained at her own disposal.

When the British became masters of Delhi, the Begum frequently visited their camp, dressed in European costume, with a hat and veil, sometimes in a palanquin, sometimes on horseback, sometimes on an elephant. At this time she appeared to be about fifty-five, was of middle height, with a beautiful complexion. Her ancient friendship for the Mahrattas, and an intercepted letter which she was believed to have written to Jeswunt Rao Holkar, caused her to be suspected by the British when they were at war with that chief in 1805. However, she succeeded in clearing herself of the accusation. The exact year of her death is not known.

Although Begum Somroo left no children of her own, she had adopted the daughter of Somroo by his first wife, a Mahratta woman. This girl wedded Mr. Dyce, a half-caste, son of Captain Dyce of the East India Company's service. The Begum had intended to make him her heir; but in her old age she detected him in a conspiracy, and so she left her property to his son, instead. This latter was the notorious David Ochterlony Dyce-Sombre. About the year 1838, this eccentric gentleman came to England, whither he had been preceded by the renown of his fabulous wealth. His arrival caused considerable excitement in London; he was fêted and invited everywhere as the lion of the day. In 1840, he married the Hon. Mary Ann Jervis, daughter of Viscount St. Vincent; but the husband and wife did not agree—a separation was speedily followed by legal proceedings against Mr. Dyce-Sombre, by which the wife's relations sought to prove the Anglo-Indian to be a lunatic. For months and months this great trial was a matter for public gossip; and the unfortunate nabob was compelled to live on the Continent for several years to escape the decision of the Court of Chancery. He returned to London in 1851, to petition against their decree; but was seized with a painful illness, of which he died on the 1st July of that year.

When Lord Lake was in India, fighting the Mahrattas, there was a Sergeant W——, of the artillery, who served in nearly all the battles of his illustrious chief. This sergeant owned a Hindoo slave, belonging to the lowest dregs of the pariahs; but through the earnest labours of a Baptist missionary, she was converted to Christianity, and the sergeant made her his wife. She accompanied him in all his campaigns, and followed him into battle. When he was tired, she would lend a hand at the guns. In one action the sergeant was struck down by a bullet which passed through his shako and struck his forehead just above the temple carrying in its course the brass hoop from the shako and forcing it into his skull. He fell, to all appearance, dead; but his wife, determined not to leave his body to the tender mercies of the foe, seized it up, and bore it from the field, amidst a rain of bullets.

The principal leaders in the terrible Indian Mutiny were Nana Sahib, Tantia Topee, and the Ranee of Jhansi. They were equally ferocious: they detested the British, and the motives which induced them to rebel were almost precisely similar. According to the laws and usages of Hindostan, a native prince, in default of sons, could adopt a strange boy and make him his heir; seldom was a dissentient voice raised against the succession of the adopted child till within the last thirty-five or forty years, when the East India Company constituted itself heir-apparent to all the thrones in the country.

The city of Jhansi is situated in Bundelcund, to the south of the river Jumna. Previous to 1857, it was the strongest and most important place in the entire of Central India. The people were nearly all Brahmins, a religion held in common with their rajahs. In the days when the Peishwa was still a person of importance in Hindostan, the ruler of Jhansi was merely a wealthy zemindar, or landowner, and he rendered such good service to the British that Lord William Bentinck (Governor-General from 1828 to 1835), raised him to the position of Rajah. On the death of this man, he was succeeded by his brother, Gungadhur Rao. The latter, having no children, made a will some weeks before his death, publicly adopting a little boy nearly related to himself, and at this time six years old. Lukshmi Baee, the Rajah's wife, was to be the guardian of this boy and Regent of Jhansi till he had attained his eighteenth year. Gungadhur gave due notice of this to the British Governor-General; and in presence of the British Resident and his assembled subjects, took the child in his lap, as a public declaration of adoption.

Gungadhur Rao died in 1854. Lord Dalhousie, the Governor-General, refused to acknowledge his right to adopt an heir, and the little province of Jhansi was annexed to British India. The young Rajah and the Ranee, his mother by adoption, were pensioned off; the latter receiving six thousand a year, paid monthly. Her troops were disbanded, and replaced by a few regiments of Sepoys and Sowars.

The Ranee was powerless to resist; she could only bide her time. She had not long to wait. Three years later, India was in a blaze. The Bundelcund Sepoys were amongst the first to mutiny. On the 14th of June, the native troops at Jhansi broke into rebellion, murdered several of their officers in the cantonments; and seized the "Star Fort." Some few English escaped to Nagoda, but the rest, numbering fifty-five men, women, and children, barricaded themselves in the "Town Fort." But after a brave resistance of four days, the mutineers burst open the gates on the 8th; and the English, having been promised life and liberty, laid down their arms. Thereupon a massacre commenced, which for barbarity, almost equalled that which took place shortly after at Cawnpore. Nineteen ladies, twenty-three children, twenty-four civil service employés, two non-commissioned officers, and eight officers were butchered in a manner familiar to all who can remember the Indian Mutiny.

It was generally believed at the time that this massacre took place by order of the Ranee, who is said to have stood by while the heads of ladies were chopped off, and the brains of babies were dashed out upon the flags. Nay, some have declared she laughed aloud when some deed of atrocity worse than the rest came under her notice.

Shortly after this massacre, the Ranee took the field at the head of some hundreds of Sepoys, and marched towards Gwalior, where Scindiah, the descendant of our old enemy whom we routed at Assaye, remained faithful to the British. But little was known of her movements during the rest of 1857; in August of that year, a female, dressed in a green uniform, was captured at Delhi, while leading on a party of Sepoys. This woman was at first supposed to be the terrible Ranee, and a rumour sped through the British Camp that she was leading the Gwalior rebels; but it was afterwards found that Lukshmi Baee still remained in the territories of the Maharajah. The prisoner was described as "an ugly old woman, short and fat." She was a species of prophetess, held in high estimation by the rebels around Delhi.

In January, 1858, Sir Hugh Rose (Lord Strathnairn), commanding the second brigade of the Central India Field Force, set out against the rebels south of Delhi; his chief object being the capture of Jhansi. Having been joined by Brigadier Stuart, they invested the fortress on the 21st of March following.

The city of Jhansi measured about four miles and a half in circumference. It stood on a level plain, surrounding the east, north, and part of the south sides of an elevated rock on which the fort stood. Altogether it was a fine specimen of modern fortification; and since the first outbreak of the Mutiny, its strength had been considerably added to by the Ranee, who took care to arm the batteries with heavy ordnance of long range. On the 25th a tremendous cannonade was opened from the British lines. Throughout the siege the intrepid Ranee tried every means to defend the town; all through the day she remained in the fort directing the fire of the artillerymen, save when she visited the different points of defence, watching and planning to strengthen the weak parts of her entrenchments.

Tantia Topee marched to the relief of Jhansi with twenty or twenty-five thousand men, and an obstinately contested battle was fought on the 1st of April.

But Tantia Topee, after proving himself to be a brave man and an able general, was totally routed with the loss of all his ordnance.

Next day a general assault was made on the city; under a murderous fire the British forced their way through the streets. When they had more than half conquered it, the news of the Ranee's flight put an end to all further resistance on the part of the rebels. It was then found that the brave old tigress, utterly disheartened by the defeat of Tantia Topee, had fled during the previous night, under cover of the darkness. Followed by about three hundred rebels, she joined Tantia Topee at Koonch. Sir Hugh Rose, as soon as he had settled matters in Jhansi, directed his march towards Calpee. He was intercepted at Koonch by the Ranee and her ally; when a spirited action took place on the 9th of May. The mutineers were driven from their entrenched camp, with great loss, and the town fell into the hands of the victors. Tantia Topee and the Ranee fled to Calpee, where they were besieged on the 16th by Sir Hugh; Calpee fell on the 23rd, the Ranee and Tantia having previously retired towards Gwalior. The Maharajah, refusing to join the rebels, was driven to take refuge in the British cantonments at Agra.

On the approach of Sir Hugh Rose, Tantia Topee fled, leaving the Ranee to defend the city. But she was not a woman easily dispirited. She disposed her forces (chiefly composed of the Gwalior Contingent) most skilfully, so as to command all the roads leading to Gwalior. She was scarcely ever out of the saddle; dressed in a sowar's uniform, and attended by a picked, well-armed escort, she rode from post to post, superintending all the operations.

Sir Hugh Rose reached the Moorar cantonments on the 16th of June, and carried them with but slight loss. To intercept his reinforcements, the Ranee marched to the banks of the little river Oomrar. Brigadiers Smith and Orr, who were marching from Antree to join in the attack on Gwalior, reached Kota-ki-Serai, on the banks of this stream, on the morning of the 17th. Between this village and Gwalior, from which it is distant about three or four miles, the road winds through a succession of hilly ranges. Some rebel pickets were observed in front of and below the first range; a squadron of the 8th Hussars immediately crossed the stream to reconnoitre, when they were fired upon from a masked battery. Two troops of the same regiment were ordered to charge; and riding at full speed through a narrow ravine, they captured a battery armed with three guns. Thence they pressed on to the rebel camp, where the enemy was driven to bay. The Ranee of Jhansi and her sister, both in the dress of sowars, fought desperately, and lost their lives in a gallant charge made to check the British troopers.

The Ranee's death was caused either by the bullet of a British rifleman, or by the fragment of a shell which pierced her breast. Her body was never found; it was said to have been burned by her followers immediately after the battle.

Upon her death the rebel hosts melted like snow before a sunbeam. The British infantry speedily carried the first range of heights; and the enemy, after losing about four hundred men, and seeing their camp in flames, were compelled to fly. The British, after losing about fifteen men (ten of whom died from sunstroke and fatigue), and spiking three rebel guns, resumed their march; and the same evening rejoined Sir Hugh Rose. The combined forces now advanced on Gwalior, routed the sepoys in the battle of Gurrowlee, June 19th, and recaptured the city, June 20th, when Scindiah was restored to his throne.

The death of the Ranee excited very little interest in this country. The newspapers of the time, with but one or two exceptions, barely chronicled the event, without making any comments; but it was universally felt by every British soldier serving in India that, with the death of Lukshmi Baee, we had lost the foe who was able to do us most injury. For courage and military skill she was acknowledged to be far superior to any of the other rebel chiefs. The message flashed along the wires announcing that the Ranee had fallen, added that "the deaths of Moulvie and the Ranee were more gain to us than half-a-dozen victories."

The exact age of the "Indian Boadicea" was never accurately determined. While one journal styles her "this girl, barely twenty years of age," another assumes her age to have been at least thirty. An employé of the East India Company who visited Jhansi in 1854, and accidentally caught a glimpse of this oriental heroine, describes her as "a woman of about the middle size—rather stout, but not *too* stout. Her face" he says, "must have been very handsome when she was younger, and even now it had many charms—though, according to my idea of beauty, it was too round. The expression, also, was very good and very intellectual. The eyes were particularly fine, and the nose very delicately shaped. She was not very fair, though she was far from black. What spoilt her was her voice, which was something between a whine and a croak."

All agreed as to the extreme licentiousness and immorality of her habits; and the rooms in her palace are said to have been hung with pictures "such as pleased Tiberius at Capri."

It was formerly the custom with many of the native princes to maintain female warriors to guard their zenanas. The tyrant Ferokshere, who was murdered in 1719, kept up an Amazon corps at Delhi, composed of Abyssinians, Cashmerians, Persians--in short, drawn from every nation whence slaves could be easily procured. They were armed with matchlocks, bows and arrows, spears and targets, and other weapons, according to their nationality. When the Emperor took refuge from his assailants in the zenana, the female guards held the entrance bravely for some time, and exchanged shots with the rebels; but they received more wounds than they gave, and were so easily driven away.

In the harem of the Nizam, at Hyderabad, there was, so lately as the time of the Mutiny, a regiment of Amazons who wore scarlet tunics, green trousers, and red cloth hats, trimmed with gold lace and mounted with a green plume. Their arms were the customary musket and bayonet. Whenever a distinguished foreigner visited the Palace, the female guard received him with military honours. "The extreme youth, and delicate appearance of these interesting warriors," says Prince Soltykoff, "at once attracted attention." Though, despite these feminine attractions, he says their aspect was so decidedly military, he would never have known they were females but for their long hair and the fulness of their bosoms. Their hair was tied in a knot, though in place of concealing it under their caps, they let it fall over the collar of their tunics.

An interesting sketch of the female sepoys at Lucknow is given in the "Private Life of an Eastern King."

"Of the living curiosities of the Palace, there were none the account of which will appear more strange to European ears than the female sepoys. I had seen these men-like women pacing up and down before the various entrances to the female apartments for many days before I was informed of their real character. I regarded them simply as a diminutive race of soldiers with well wadded coats. There was nothing but that fulness of the chest to distinguish many of them from other sepoys; and one is so accustomed to see soldiers in England with coats stuffed so as to make their wearers resemble pouter-pigeons, that I took little heed of the circumstance.

"These women retained their long hair, which they tied up in a knot on the top of the head, and there it was concealed by the usual shako. They bore the ordinary accoutrements of sepoys in India—the musket and bayonet, cross-belts and cartridge-boxes, jackets and white duck continuations, which might be seen anywhere in Bengal. Intended solely for duty in the Palace as guardians of the harem, they were paraded only in the court-yards, where I have seen them going through their exercise just like other sepoys. They were drilled by one of the native officers of the king's army, and appeared quite familiar with marching and wheeling, with presenting, loading, and firing muskets, with the fixing and unfixing of bayonets; in fact, with all the detail of the ordinary barrack-yard. Whether they could have gone through the same marches in the field with thousands of mustachioed sepoys around them, I cannot tell—probably not. They had their own corporals and sergeants; none of them, I believe, attained a higher rank than that of sergeant.

"Many of them were married women, obliged to quit the ranks for a month or two at a time, occasionally. They retained their places, however, as long as possible. .... Of these female sepoys there were in all two companies of the usual strength, or weakness, if the reader will have it so. Once, during my residence at Lucknow, they were employed by the king against his own mother."

This act of Nussir was rendered all the worse, because many years before, when Ghazi-u-deen, the late King of Oude, wished to disinherit his son and put him to death, the Begum armed her retainers, and fought for Nussir with the courage of a lion. After many had fallen on each side, the British resident interfered, and put an end to the contest. Nussir, after he became king, wished to act towards his son as Ghazi would have done towards him; but the old Begum now fought as stoutly for her grandson as she did previously for her son. The King sent his female sepoys to turn her out of her palace, but she armed her servants, fought the sepoys, and put them to flight. Fifteen or sixteen of the Begum's adherents were left dead on the field. The resident again interfered, and guaranteed the life and succession of the child.

But Nussir succeeded in cheating his mother after all, by declaring the boy illegitimate. In vain the old Begum, after the death of Nussir, surrounded the British Residency with her troops; the Englishman was not to be intimidated. Troops were ordered up from the cantonments, and a few discharges of grape quickly dispersed the Begum's adherents. One of Nussir's uncles was then placed on the throne, and the brave old Begum was compelled to submit.

There is a similar guard of female warriors in the Palace of the King of Siam, at Bangkok; and the Paris papers of September, 1866, speak of a regiment of female Zouaves, armed with rifles, which was then being raised in the first-named city.

As lately as 1873, we read of Amazonian soldiers in Bantam. Says a newspaper of that date, describing the condition of the sexes in that kingdom:— "Although tributary to Holland, it is an independent state, politically without importance, yet happy, rich, and since time immemorial governed and defended by women. The sovereign is indeed a man, but all the rest of the government belongs to the fair sex. The king is entirely dependent upon his state council, composed of three women. The highest authorities, all state officers, court functionaries, military commanders, and soldiers are, without exception, of the female sex. The men are agriculturists and merchants. The body-guard of the king is formed of the female *élite*. These amazons ride in the masculine style, wearing sharp steel points instead of spurs. They carry a pointed lance, which they swing very gracefully, and also a musket, which is discharged at full gallop. The throne is inheritable by the eldest son, and in case the king dies without issue a hundred elected amazons assemble, in order to choose a successor from among their own sons. The chosen one is then proclaimed lawful king."

VI.

SAVAGE AFRICA.—Judith, Queen of Abyssinia—Workite and Mastrat, Gallas Queens—Shinga, Queen of Congo—Mussasa, Queen of Matamba — Tembandumba, Queen of the Jagas — Amazons in Dahomey.

THE great African continent has contributed but little to the pages of history. Centuries before America was discovered, northern Africa was one of the centres of commerce, its people were amongst the most civilized in the known world; yet America has been explored in almost every part, from north to south, and its history is as well known and almost as full of interest as that of Europe or Asia, while Africa, until within the last three-quarters of a century, remained, geographically and historically, almost as much a mystery as it was in ancient times. Rightly has it been styled the Dark Continent.

Ethiopia, renowned in distant eras for its stately cities adorned with lofty temples and spacious palaces, and inhabited by learned men, is a sad picture of fallen greatness. Its haughty palaces have crumbled to decay long since, and their sites are occupied by the mud cabins of a savage race, who, only for being Christians, differ very little from their fellow-men who dwell on other parts of this great continent. People took but small interest in Abyssinia till the war with King Theodore, and even then we learned very little more about that strange land than our grandfathers told us.

Scarcely more than a bare outline of Abyssinian history has been preserved; yet we find that, since the days of the Queen of Sheba, women have more than once taken an active part in the politics of this kingdom. Bruce has given us the story of a beautiful Jewish women named Judith, who, with the aid of her co-religionists, usurped the throne in the 10th or 11th century. She was the wife of Gideon, the governor, or, as he might be called, the feudal sovereign, of a small district called Bugna. He was also a Jew, as were all his subjects. Judith at last grew so powerful that she resolved to overthrow the Christians. She accordingly surprised the almost impregnable rock Damo, where the royal princes were kept for safety, and slew them to the number of four hundred. Del Naad, the King, at this time a mere child, was saved by some of the nobles, who carried him into the loyal province of Shoa. Judith then mounted the throne, and not only reigned over Abyssinia for upwards of forty years, but transmitted the throne to five successive descendants. After that, the line of King Solomon and the Queen of Sheba, as represented by the descendants of Del Naad, was restored.

Even in these degenerate days, women sometimes come forward as leaders in Abyssinia. After the fall of Magdala, Lord Napier was visited by the two Gallas queens, Workite (gold), and Mastrat (looking-glass), who had a race as to which should first congratulate the British general on his victory. These rival queens, who have been fighting one another for years past, professed great delight at the reception which they met with, and both gave and received presents in token of friendship. The *Times* Correspondent in Abyssinia gave a lively and amusing description of them:—

"I am told on good authority," he wrote, "that they go into battle, and handle spear, sword, and gun right manfully; there is even a story, probably mythical, that Mastrat with her own hand wounded the mighty Theodore. But usually they go about so muffled up, and looking so like a bundle of shawls moved by mechanism, that, except in their method of riding, their appearance is anything but amazonic. Workite kept herself closely wrapped up, and hidden during her stay in camp, but Mastrat boldly threw aside her rich royal robe of crimson, speckled with gold, and came out of her tent, and before the soldiers—if her majesty will pardon the expression—like a man, to have her photograph taken. Her complexion was a very pale olive—fairer than that of many Europeans—and her expression, though the features were large, and scarcely, like those of Theodore's widow-in-chief, of the thoroughbred type, were essentially queen-like and commanding. She looked quite capable of leading an army anywhere."

The natives of Congo, in Lower Guinea, have ever been notorious for their ferocity and love of shedding human blood; and such very savages are they, that what slight improvements have been made in their beloved pastime—war,— are due entirely to those Europeans who have visited the coast. The women are as ferocious as the men; and as the Salic law is either unknown, or neglected, there have from time to time been female sovereigns renowned for their military prowess.

One of these royal Amazons was Shinga, or Zingha, Queen of Matamba, in Congo, who ascended the throne on the death of her brother about 1640. She determined to be Queen in her own dominions, and set herself up as a stern opponent of Christianity. She thereby offended the Portuguese priests (who had been established in the country since 1487), and they stirred up her nephew to rebellion. After losing three battles, Shinga was obliged to seek safety in flight.

After proceeding one hundred and fifty miles up the country, Shinga established a new kingdom; and by making war on the Jagas, or Giagas, the Arabs of Western Africa, she became sufficiently powerful once more to take the field against Portugal. But she was again routed, and her two sisters remained in the hands of the victors. At last, in 1646, she recovered her throne, and concluded an honourable treaty with the Christians.

Her long struggle with Portugal had so accustomed Shinga to a military life that she cared for nothing but war. She was almost constantly engaged in a campaign against the neighbouring kingdoms. Before starting on an expedition, she used to sacrifice the handsomest man she could find as a war offering to some African deity who required to be appeased. On such occasions she appeared in military costume, her bow and arrows in her hand, a sword hanging from a collar round her neck, an axe by her side. After going through a warlike dance, singing a martial song, accompanying it on two iron bells, she would cut off the victim's head as a declaration of war, and drink a deep draught of his blood.

The Jagas, at all times feared on account of their ruthless ferocity and cruelty, rose to the height of their glory under King Zimbo, who has been styled the "Napoleon of Africa." Donji, one of Zimbo's captains, was governor of Matamba; his wife, Mussusa, was a warrior like himself, and they trained their daughter, Tembandumba, to the same mode of life. After the death of Zimbo, his vast empire, like that of Alexander, was divided amongst his captains; and Donji, more skilful than the rest, conquered many of the surrounding states. After his death, Mussasa, who possessed military talent equal to her husband,—tarnished though it was by gross cruelty—continued to fight and to conquer the neighbouring chiefs.

Tembandumba received the education of a soldier. Trained, while yet a child, to the use of arms, she took naturally the trade of war. As a girl she accompanied her mother on all her campaigns; fighting side by side at the head of their troops, Mussasa and her daughter were always foremost in battle and last in a retreat. The valour and prudence of Tembandumba soon became so well known that her mother gave her the command of half the army. But when she had gained a few victories, the Amazon was not disposed to remain longer in a subordinate position. Throwing aside the authority of her mother, she assumed the title of Queen of the Jagas; and drew up a code of laws so extravagantly savage and bloodthirsty that only for the high respect, or rather terror, in which the young girl was held, even her subjects would have rebelled.

It was the ambition of Tembandumba to revive the Amazonian empire which had once existed on the African continent. In pursuance of this object, she declared war on the whole race of man; all the male children were to be slain by their mothers, and made into ointment called " Magiga Samba," which when smeared over the human body would render the latter invulnerable. The adult males throughout her dominions were to be converted into food for the women; and to prevent the tender hearts of the women causing them to evade these laws, she commanded that every other food, animal or vegetable, should be destroyed. Had her statutes been obeyed to the letter, Western Africa would soon have been a hideous wilderness, devoid of human habitations, birds, beasts, trees, plants, or even grass.

Having promulgated these laws, together with many others of minor importance, in a speech delivered before a select committee of her female subjects, she concluded by seizing her own child, who was feeding at her breast, and hurling it into a large mortar, where she beat it to a jelly. Throwing this into a large pot, she compounded an oleaginous preparation with leaves, roots and oils, which she rubbed all over her body, telling her subjects to follow the example. Such quantities of "Magiga Samba" were manufactured that travellers declare there are still some pots of it to be found among the Jagas. But after the first burst of enthusiasm was over, maternal love prevailed, and Tembandumba, after vainly endeavouring, by the appointment of inspectors, to enforce obedience, was obliged to repeal the law, and permit children taken in war to be substituted to make the precious ointment.

For many years this female devil reigned triumphantly; she kept the Jagas so constantly engrossed by martial glory, they had no time to sigh for liberty. Kingdom after kingdom fell before her legions; wherever she turned her footsteps, a track of desolation remained to mark her progress.

But Tembandumba, after all, was not above the weaknesses common to her sex; all her passions were exaggerated, and, like many another heroine, she owed her final overthrow to the God of Love. As a rule she caused her husbands to be treated as Schahriar, in the Arabian Nights, used his wives; but at last she fell really in love with Culemba, a private in the army. Culemba was young, strong, and decidedly good-looking—for a negro. He possessed insinuating manners, and succeeded for a time in gaining some influence over the Queen. But in time she wearied of him, as she had grown tired of her former lovers. Culemba, knowing by experience that she had an unpleasant fancy for dining off her lovers, was determined to be beforehand with her. He was a cruel, ambitious man,—equally crafty as Tembandumba. He invited the Queen to a sumptuous banquet; such an invitation being the highest compliment one Jaga could pay to another. The entertainment was magnificent, the wine delicious; but while drinking a bumper of Lisbon wine from the skull of an old enemy, the Queen of the Jagas fell down dead.

Culemba was—of course—inconsolable. With difficulty could he be prevented from slaying himself on the corpse. The funeral was conducted with all the splendour customary at the interment of a native African sovereign; the dead queen was buried in a large vault excavated on the top of a high hill. The corpse was placed in a commanding attitude on a throne, surrounded by skins, stuffs, mats, ostrich feathers, and all her favourite dishes and liquors.

Dahomey—or, as it is now fashionable to style it, Dahomé—may with truth be called one of the greatest curiosities of the Nineteenth Century. It seems so strange that a large, closely populated country, the monarch of which is anxious to cultivate the friendship of Europe, should be sunk in such gross barbarity. The chief features of its government are the Slave-Trade, the "Customs," or religious festivals, at which the notorious human sacrifices are offered, and the Amazons; and the last are by far the greatest curiosity. Very few rulers, in ancient or modern times, have authorised the keeping up a standing army of women; and none of the native tribes along the coast seem at all inclined to follow the example of Dahomey.

But the female sex in Dahomey is, they say, vastly superior to the male; the women are tall—upwards of six feet high, and powerfully built—the men, on the contrary, are, as a general rule, round-limbed and sickly-looking. Captain Burton suggests that it was this physical superiority which originated the custom of employing women-soldiers.

The Amazonian division of the army numbers twelve thousand women, ready at an hour's notice for active service. They are officered by females, and have a female commander-in-chief, who is entirely independent of the "Gau" or male commander-in-chief. To denote her rank, this female general wears a silver horn, hammer-shaped, projecting from her forehead, similar to a unicorn. The officers are distinguished by a white head-cloth, and by the superior make and material of their clothes; and when on the march, they are attended by what Captain Burton styles an "esquiress" or slave-girl, who carries the musket of her mistress.

The honorary captaincy of each corps is presented by the King to one of his sons, after whom it is sometimes named; though the companies are as frequently styled by the name of the district to which they specially belong. Sometimes the King presents some distinguished European traveller whom he wishes to compliment, with a honorary command.

The Amazons are not remarkable for any superfluity of muscle, but as a rule they are lithe and active. As they grow older, many become extremely stout. "Some of them" remarks Captain Burton "are prodigies of obesity." The commander-in-chief, he says, was "vast in breadth." Beauty is scarce in Dahomey, and what little there is, has not fallen to the lot of the Amazons. Captain Burton, who "expected to see Penthesileas, Thalestrises, Dianas," was sadly disappointed when he beheld "old, ugly, and square-built frows, trudging 'grumpily' along, with the face of 'cook' after being much 'nagged' by the 'missus'." They do not, however, as was once supposed, condemn themselves to single-blessedness; on the contrary, many have husbands and children.

They are very careful of their weapons—an English "Tower-marked" firelock, a short falchion, or dirk, and a large razor for cutting off heads.

The musket is guarded by numerous charms, and when not in use is protected from the damp by a black, monkey-skin case; the barrel is polished bright, and sometimes adorned with a long tassel. Their skill in the use of these weapons is such as to render them exceedingly formidable adversaries.

Their uniforms are very showy. That of the Royal Guard—which, numbering rather more than a thousand women, is always stationed about the King's person—consists of a sleeveless tunic, surtout, or waistcoat of different colours, buttoning down the front, a pink, blue, or yellow loin-wrapper, or kilt, reaching to the ancles, a sash, generally white, tied round the waist, and folding down in two long ends on the left side, and a fillet of blue or white cotton round the head. The arms are left bare. A black leather belt, with cartridge box—or "agluadya"—forms a girdle, with holds the surtout tight to the figure. This belt is sometimes ornamented with cowrie shells; on it are hung bandoleers, which contain, in separate compartments, twelve, sixteen, or even twenty wooden powder-boxes. Each cartridge contains about four times the quantity of powder used in English cartridges, and the bullet is not placed in it as in Europe; a small leather ball-bag hangs from the shoulder by a strap which passes through the belt. When the Amazons are loading, they pour the powder into the barrel without any wadding, and then drop in a bullet, or a few slugs.

Shaving the head is a general, though not a universal fashion. Those who do so, leave only a small tuft of hair like a cockade; others, however, who do not follow this custom, shave a narrow strip, two inches in breadth, from the forehead to the crown of the head.

When the Amazons are on the march, the privates are obliged to carry an immense number of articles absolutely necessary for a campaign under the scorching sun of Africa. Packs, containing their bed-mats, a change of clothes, and food for a fortnight—said food consisting of toasted grains or bean cakes spiced with pepper—small stools with three or four legs, two cartridge-boxes, water-gourds, fetish-sacks, powder-calabashes, bullet-wallets, fans, wooden pipe-cases, leather tobacco-bags, hats made of felt or straw, and palm-leaf umbrellas, are just a few of the things carried by them on the march.

The King of Dahomey is very proud of his female soldiers, whom he frequently passes in review. He regards these Amazonian field-days with a pride akin to that of Frederick the Great at one of the Potzdam Reviews, or Napoleon at a review of his Old Guard.

These grand reviews are very showy, effective sights. Although the discipline is not very exact, yet the evolutions performed are executed with a vigour and heartiness which almost atone for the lack of that neatness observed in more civilized armies. The King seats himself under a canopy in some public place, generally the market-place of the town, and the various corps of Amazons march on to the open ground in front; each regiment being preceded by its band, playing the most discordant music on fantastically shaped instruments made of elephant's-trunks, bullock's-horns, and triangular iron tubes (which, when struck, emit a sound similar to a sheep-bell), and beating a large war-drum in a truly deafening manner. This drum, ornamented with twelve human skulls, is carried on the head of one Amazon, while another walks after, beating it. Each corps possesses a similar drum, adorned with a like number of skulls. Every company has, likewise, six or seven standards, the top of each being surmounted by a human skull. In the more disciplined regiments, there is always an advance-guard of nine women, followed, at a short interval, by fifty supports.

The ceremony of passing them in review is so elaborate that one corps has occupied as much as two or three hours before being disposed of. According as each corps arrives within a short distance of the Royal canopy, a halt is ordered, and the women lie down, or squat down, to await their turn to appear before his majesty. The captain then introduces the officers by name, and all kneel down, throwing up the light red dust in showers over themselves. Their deeds of valour are recounted, and when any warrior has especially distinguished herself, the King graciously bestows his royal praises. After all have been noticed, the officers fall into their proper places, and, together with the privates, burst into a complimentary song in honour of their ruler. It is usual for various Amazons, on the conclusion of this song, to step one after another to the front, and declare their loyalty. Then the entire corps kneels down, with the butt ends of their muskets resting on the ground, and the barrel slanting back over the shoulder. After covering themselves once more with dust, they poise their muskets horizontally in both hands, and, still on their knees, pour forth a lusty cheer. Then springing to their feet with another hearty cheer, they slope arms, and set off at the double-quick march, each trying to outstrip the rest.

This part of the review having at last concluded, the Amazons march on to an open space where sham entrenchments have been constructed. These mock fortifications usually consist of two or three great piles of green briar, armed with the most dangerous kind of prickly thorns. This thorny briar is much used in Africa, and formerly was employed in Asia, to entrench villages or towns. The clumps are about seventy feet wide and eight feet high, standing perhaps three hundred yards in advance of several pens, or yards, the latter surrounded by a strong wall about seven feet high, defended by dense masses of thorns, thickly matted with reeds. To defend this mock entrenchment, a few dozen royal slaves are placed within the enclosure.

Each corps, as it marches on to the ground, headed by the officer appointed to lead the attack—who wears a sword of a different shape from the others—halts about two hundred yards from the nearest pile, and shoulders arms. Directly the signal is given, they charge over the thorns, regardless of their bare feet, and in less than a minute the mimic fortress is captured. At intervals of twenty minutes, the other corps have captured the remaining piles, and they all return in triumph, each leading a slave by a rope. On reaching the royal canopy, each Amazon presents a scalp supposed to have been taken during the sham fight.

Sometimes the Amazons are rehearsed in volley-firing and target-practice. They load and fire quickly, singing all the time. Their target-practice is moderately good. Several thousand goats are tied to stakes in a large field surrounded by a mud wall about ten feet high. Most of the goats are killed before the day is over; which, when we take into account the indifferent quality of their powder, and the careless manner in which they load, speaks very well for the Amazons as markswomen.

The King of Dahomey is almost always engaged in some war, whether foreign or domestic; therefore a few hundred Amazons are constantly on active service. Like the Old Guard, the services of these female warriors are never brought into use save in cases of dire necessity, or when considerable opposition is expected. As the Amazons always strive not only to behead, but to scalp their enemies, they are pretty sure of having one or more of these ghastly trophies to show the King on their return from a campaign. Scalps, however, do not accumulate so fast as one might suppose; six or seven in a year is considered rather a large number, for the Amazons are frequently obliged, after slaying a foe, to pass on without securing his topknot.

The Slave-trade provides very constant exercise for the Amazons; because, whenever the King requires slaves, it is necessary to go to war with some neighbour—though of course, his Majesty easily finds a *casus belli*. But the great thorn of vexation in the royal side for the past thirty years and more has been the republic of Abbeokuta. The influence of this free state, in destroying the slave-trade, very naturally brought down the hatred of the King of Dahomey, who is the largest dealer in human flesh on the African coast. More than once he has tried to conquer this sturdy little city. On the 3rd of March, 1851, he appeared before the walls of Abbeokuta at the head of a great army— male and female. A furious attack was made to gain the ramparts, but the rapid, murderous fire of the Egbas drove back the Dahomans with fearful slaughter, and put them to rout. The Amazons led the attack; many were slain—nearly all the slain Dahomans were women—and one or two made prisoners.

The King undertook a second expedition against Abbeokuta in March, 1864. At the head of ten thousand picked warriors, and three brass six-pounders, he arrived before the walls on the 16th. The Amazons formed the column of attack, and displayed their accustomed bravery. Directly the signal was given for the assault, they scaled the wall like furies, and for a time threatened to carry everything before them. One Amazon having her right hand cut off, clung to the parapet and killed her adversary with her left, before being hurled back into the ditch.

The Egbas received the Amazons with a murderous fire, which thinned their ranks terribly. They were obliged to seek safety in flight, and their example was speedily followed by the whole Dahoman army. The Egbas, sallying forth, pursued the retreating foe, massacring the stragglers without mercy. In this congenial task they were joined by the neighbouring tribes, who turned out in great numbers and joined heartily in the carnage.

The King of Dahomey experienced a most disastrous rout, with the loss of three thousand of of his best soldiers, one thousand being slain, and two thousand taken prisoners.

THE END.

PRINTED BY TAYLOR AND CO.,
10, LITTLE QUEEN STREET, LINCOLN-INN-FIELDS.

www.ingramcontent.com/pod-product-compliance
Lightning Source LLC
Chambersburg PA
CBHW031818220426
43662CB00007B/696